W9-BTN-911

Live! Love! Laugh!
Father Charlie

Dreams Really Do Come True!

by Father Charlie Urnick

ISBN: 1456311727
ISBN-13: 9781456311728

This is a collection of sermons given at St. John the Baptist Catholic Church in Laughlin, Nevada from July 2008 until July 2009. To hear the current sermons, please join us for Mass. We love company! Our Weekend Mass schedule is as follows:

Saturday   4:00 PM
Mass at Don's Celebrity Theatre
in the Riverside Resort

Saturday   6:00 PM
Mass at St. John the Baptist Catholic Church

Sunday   8:00 AM
Mass at St. John the Baptist Catholic Church

Sunday   10:00 AM
Mass at Don's Celebrity Theatre
in the Riverside Resort

Sunday   12:00 Noon
Mass at Don's Celebrity Theatre
in the Riverside Resort

St. John the Baptist Catholic Church
P.O. Box 31230
Laughlin   Nevada   89028

❖ ❖ ❖

OFFICE OF
THE BISHOP
(702) 735-9805
FAX (702) 735-8941

Diocese of Las Vegas

P.O. BOX 18316
LAS VEGAS, NEVADA 89114-8316

December 16, 2010

Father Charles Urnick
Administrator
St. John the Baptist Catholic Church
P. O. Box 31230
Laughlin, NV 89028

Dear Father Urnick:

After consultation with Right Reverend Archimandrite Francis Vivona, Censor Librorum for the Diocese of Las Vegas, I give you ecclesiastical approval for the book *"Dreams Really Do Come True"* for public use among the faithful.

Nihil Obstat:	Right Reverend Archimandrite Francis Vivona, STM, JCL
Imprimatur:	Most Reverend Joseph A. Pepe, D.D., J.C.D.
Date:	December 16, 2010

Wishing you the best, I remain

Sincerely yours in Christ,

+ *Joseph A. Pepe*

Most Reverend Joseph A. Pepe, D.D., J.C.D.
Bishop of Las Vegas

JAP/pb

C: Right Reverend Archimandrite Francis M. Vivona, S.T.M., J.C.L.

To all those who read this book -

I am the happiest Catholic priest in the whole world! I am in my 36th year as a priest and my current assignment is Paradise, otherwise known as Laughlin, Nevada! I have been assigned here as Administrator of St. John the Baptist Catholic Church since July 1, 2008. The title of my book comes directly from my views about this assignment: **DREAMS REALLY DO COME TRUE!** As far back as I can remember, my dream has been to serve as a priest in the Diocese of Las Vegas, and here I am living my dream along the banks of the beautiful Colorado River!

I have always been blessed with happiness because of the amazing people in my life, and since this book is the first one I have ever written (but hopefully not the last!), I really want and need to single out some of those amazing people for praise and thanks:

My Mom and Dad who brought me into this world a long time ago. My Dad lived to see me almost complete my teenage years. He died in 1967. My Mom lived to see me ordained as a priest and shared so much of my love for Las Vegas and Nevada throughout the years. Mom died in 2006, but she is very much a part of my life even now.

The parishioners of St. John the Baptist Catholic Parish in Laughlin, Nevada, who give me so much hope and joy and love, and who have to listen to me preach almost every weekend of the year! I first called Laughlin "Paradise" in my sermon on 23 November 2008! And it will be "Paradise" forever in my mind until I get to the OTHER Paradise (Heaven)!

The snowbirds and visitors who come to Laughlin from all over the world and who worship with us either at our church on the hill or in the Riverside casino, and who bring me bulletins and news from churches around the world.

My brother Michael who really has been the behind-the-scenes force in my life, always encouraging me to be my best self, patiently calling me to account when I am not, and inspiring me to see and hear elements of life I might never have noticed without him. Many times he has had to "take one for the team", but it is undeniably true that it is to Michael that I owe the push to actually sit down and write this book. Michael is first mentioned as a friend in the sermon of 26 October 2008, but he is really and truly the best brother a guy could ever have! Michael, I'm so blessed and so glad we're family!

My "illegitimate son" Eddie who shows up on several pages of this book because his genuine goodness and youthful enthusiasm make me the proudest Pa in the world. Eddie is first mentioned in the sermon of 8 February 2009 as a friend, but by the sermon of 21 June 2009, he is clearly my much-loved illegitimate son! There's an old saying that if you love someone, you sometimes want to kill him.

I love you, son! (NLPLC) Eddie, I'm so blessed and so glad we're family!

My weird nephew Andy who recently discovered his Vegas family on his way to LA. He doesn't show up in this book because he only came on the scene in 2010, but he will definitely have a place in the future ones! Andy, I'm so blessed and so glad we're family!

My friends Paul and Charlie who keep me honest and truthful and smiling. I don't think they realize how much their friendship has contributed to my life, but I owe them big time, really big time! They are really the very first friends I made in Las Vegas when I moved out West.

My friend Bruce whose own writings online are so good and so inspirational for me to read and who shares a beautiful outlook on life and grace with me.

The priests of my past who taught me so much by their preaching, and so much more by their lives: Father Charlie O'Connor, Msgr. Tom Kleissler, Father Ed Duffy, Father Gerry McGarry, Msgr. Dave Casazza, Father Francis Byrne, Father Ken St. Amand, Msgr. James Turro, Father Chuck McCusker, Father Charlie Hudson, Msgr. Peter O'Connor, Msgr. Caesar Orrico, Msgr. Mike Fitzpatrick, Msgr. Charles Lillis, Father Robert Hunt, Father Ed Ciuba, Msgr. Harold Darcy, Father Steve Feehan, Msgr. Carl Hinrichsen, and Father Edward Hinds.

And all those people who have said to me on their way out of Mass here in Laughlin: **"Have you ever thought of putting your sermons together in a book?"** Well, now I have!

I began serious work on this collection of sermons from my first year in Laughlin on February 14, 2010, and I completed the basic structure on October 17, 2010, spending almost eight months revising and revisiting a year of sermons at St. John the Baptist Catholic Church in Laughlin. It has definitely been a labor of love doing this! For those who hear me regularly, you will recognize the development of some common themes and messages. You will see some wonderfully awesome recurring characters in my sermons because they are in my life. I never have to make up my stories, they happen to me!

Welcome to my world!

Most of my sermon material is purely original, but sometimes it has been inspired by things I have seen or read in books, magazines, newspapers and on the internet. I apologize if I have inadvertently used someone else's material without giving proper credit. I do occasionally read sermon ideas by Father Anthony Kadavil online and *A World of Stories for Preachers and Teachers* by William J. Bausch provided one of the stories in this book.

A portion of the profits from the sale of this book ($1.00 from every book sold) will be donated to St. John the Baptist Catholic Church to assist in the current works and activities of the best little parish in the world! We are proud to be a little outpost of the Diocese of Las Vegas serving all those who live in or visit Laughlin, and the surrounding communities in Nevada, Arizona, and California.

Over the years, I've collected a number of sayings which I have found to be helpful, humorous, thoughtful and guiding. I gladly share them with you at the start of this journey which begins with my first sermon in Laughlin and spans the entire year that follows. Perhaps reading some of these sayings might prepare you for the mind and spirit behind the sermons that follow. I hope you enjoy the journey with me, it's going to be an awesome ride!

"I wouldn't like to have lived without ever having disturbed anyone!" (Catherine Doherty)

"Relationships are built on trust; trust begins by sharing." (Christian Mueller)

"Laughter is the sound of assumptions breaking." (Michael Goudeau)

"For personal growth, you should do something every day that scares you!" (Kevin Lynch...as he coaxed me onto his Harley!)

"Consider any man that you can help your friend, and double friend that man so selfless as to offer help to you." (Rod McKuen)

"We are all molded and remolded by those who have loved us, and though that love may pass we remain, nonetheless, their work.....No love, no friendship can ever cross the path of our destiny without leaving some mark upon it forever." (Francois Mauriac)

"You are loved!" (Arthur Walters)

"I think when you are somewhere, you oughta be there, 'cause it's not about how long you stay in a place, it's about what you do while you're there. And when you go, will the place where you've been be any better off for your having been there? (Chris Stevens/John Corbett in the show "Northern Exposure")

"Someday, we'll look back on this, laugh nervously, and change the subject!" (Ken Mason)

"Live!...Love!...Laugh!" (David Kesterson)

"There is nothing wrong with pointing out the flaws of people you care about as long as you are in their lives long enough to assist them in overcoming their flaws." (Michael Rene Serrano, 25 July 2009)

"Of course you did!"....."Really?" (Michael Rene Serrano)

"You're stuck with me - wherever I go, whatever I do - you're coming along for the ride!" (Eddie Gelhaus, 29 March 2010))

"Haha! I'll deny the stories and burn the pics!" (Andy Greene, 30 September 2010)

"Pray for me! What harm could it do?" (Father Charlie)

"See you in church!" (Father Charlie)

"Be good, be strong, be you!" (Father Charlie)

"Dreams really do come true! (Father Charlie)

❖ ❖ ❖

14th Sunday in Ordinary Time - "A"

6 July 2008

FIRST READING: Zechariah 9:9-10
PSALM: Psalm 145:1-2, 8-11, 13-14
SECOND READING: Romans 8:9, 11-13
GOSPEL: Matthew 11:25-30

In the Gospel today, Jesus is at home, and He invites all to come to Him where they will find rest.

According to the news reports, the 4th of July week-end is one of the busiest in terms of the number of people traveling by air as well as by car all over the country. **I love to travel!** And I've gotten to see some really exciting places in my life so far. I've seen the pyramids and the Great Sphinx in Egypt. I even got to ride a camel (smelly, but fun!). I've climbed a volcano in Mexico. I've seen boiling hot springs in Iceland, and ancient ruins in Turkey, and ancient civilizations in Hong Kong. I've watched giant sea turtles along the Great Barrier Reef in Australia and I've cuddled a koala there too. I've visited every state in the USA with the exception of North Dakota.....and someday I will see North Dakota! **I REALLY LOVE TO TRAVEL!** And I suspect that Jesus loved to travel too. So many of the Gospels are about His journeys throughout Judea, Samaria and Galilee. They tell us of the miraculous cures He worked, the people He visited, the teachings He gave in the various places He visited.

But today's Gospel is different. Jesus isn't traveling all over the place. He's sitting quietly at home and talking with His disciples.

I'm really glad that we have this Gospel passage this weekend. This weekend marks my first weekend here in Laughlin as the Administrator of St. John the Baptist Catholic Church. I've been a regular visitor to Las Vegas for over 30 years. I'm born and raised in New Jersey, but I'm a huge fan of stage magic, so Las Vegas has always held a special place in my heart. There is no better place to see great stage magic! And in 1990, my Mom and I stopped in Laughlin and fell in love with the place. I even ordered a mailed subscription to the Laughlin local paper!

In 1992, when I saw that a Catholic mission was being formed here, I wrote to the first priest assigned here, Father John McShane. And three months after the mission opened in 1992, my Mom and I were here for a visit, and I covered the weekend Masses for Father John. I have been back here almost every year for the past 16 years, many of them with my Mom. In fact, the rectory here is the only rectory in Nevada where my Mom has stayed overnight. Laughlin was always a place we liked to visit (like so many of you who visit here from all over the country!). And I always told the people at the Masses, **"I'm not from here. I'm a visitor just like you!"**

This year, when I was able to transfer to the Diocese of Las Vegas, I wondered where I would be assigned. Several places were talked about, but three weeks ago, I got the word that I would be coming to Laughlin! **This is my dream come true!** And I have no doubt that my Mom, who died two years ago, had something to do with the assignment! She knew I would like living in the rectory. I know I have someone watching out for me!

I love this place so much already! They even serve fresh lemonade and fresh-baked cookies in the bank! And I've never met a buffet I didn't love! And it was so cool to have the town arrange those spectacular fireworks on Friday night to welcome me! (At least I presumed they were for me!). And the people in the mission as well as the visitors I've met have all made me feel so welcome here! So for the first time ever, I can say to you this weekend, **"This is my home, I'm glad to be here!"**

Like Jesus in today's Gospel, I'm glad to be home! And I'd like to pass on to you the same message that Jesus gave to His disciples in today's Gospel passage. He teaches them something that they can take with them wherever they go: **"I give praise to You, Father, Lord of heaven and earth, for although You have hidden these things from the wise and the learned, You have revealed them to little ones. Yes, Father, such has been Your gracious will."** And then He continues with what one of my teen-lingo-speaking friends calls "the sweetest verse in the whole New Testament": **"Come to Me, all you who labor and are burdened, and I will give you rest.....Learn from Me.....and you will find rest for yourselves."**

Here's another way to think about what I'm saying

Grandpa clocked in long hours on the railroad or in the mines or farms, but when he came home, there were no faxes or emails waiting for him to answer, no cell phone ringing to interrupt his dinner. Home was home, not a pit stop for data gathering before heading back to the office. Today, there is no downtime, no escape from other people. We have cell phones in the car, and beepers in our pockets. we carry them even to church, to the beach, and even to the bathroom. Dr. Mark Moskowitz of the Boston Medical Center comments: **"a lot of people are working 24 hours a day, 7 days a week, even when they're not technically at work. It is a guaranteed formula for breakdown."** (William J. Bausch, ed., *A World of Stories for Preachers and Teachers*, Mystic, CT: Twenty-Third Publications, 1998, page 293). I guess today's Gospel is good for them..... and for those of us who are sometimes like them.

Sometimes, when we become adults, we can try to be wise and learned, and we can forget the simple truths of childhood. Jesus promises to be with us, to reveal Himself to us. And He even invites us to come to Him with all our cares and burdens, and to lay them down and let Him give us the peace and rest that only He can give. We need time with the Lord for our sanity as well as for our salvation.

Enjoy some peaceful time this 4th of July weekend. Pray for those who are away from home defending the red, white and blue in Iraq and Afghanistan and other places all over the world. Pray that they will somehow feel the power and the peace and the presence of God in their lives wherever they may be. You and I can be here in Laughlin in peace this weekend because of the courage and faithfulness of those who in the past and in the present have defended our country. May God bless them, and may God bless us, and may God bless America on this 4th of July Weekend.

God bless you!

Father John McShane was the first priest assigned to St. John the Baptist Catholic Church in Laughlin. He came on August 15, 1992. Father Charlie Urnick is the sixth priest assigned here. He arrived on July 1, 2008.

❖ ❖ ❖

15th Sunday in Ordinary Time - "A"

13 July 2008

FIRST READING: Isaiah 55:10-11
PSALM: Psalm 65:10-14
SECOND READING: Romans 8:18-23
GOSPEL: Matthew 13:1-23

In the Gospel today, Jesus teaches the Parable of the Sower. The Sower is an image of God Who freely shares His message with all mankind.

Well, my second week here in Laughlin has been awesome! I know I've eaten much too much! The week began on Monday morning when one of the parishioners brings a frosted lemon cake to church. And having two pieces of frosted lemon cake before 9:00 AM sure sets the tone for the week! And then there was the CINNABON that was dropped off, and the seafood buffet later in the week.....I was thinking of getting into shape out here in Laughlin, but I have a feeling that the only shape I'm going to be getting in out here is ROUND!

Besides eating a lot this week, plants have been on my mind a lot. I've been looking for a saguaro cactus because it has always been one of my favorite-looking plants. I have this idea of finding a big one, even an artificial one, and hanging Christmas lights on it in December and having it as my Christmas tree out here in the desert. Now that would be a picture to send back to my friends in New Jersey!

Speaking of plants, I have found that there are only two types of plants that I can successfully grow and they are the exact opposite of one another. I can grow cactus which requires no care and almost no water, and I can grow bamboo, which lives in water. In fact, I once had my cactus and my bamboo right next to one another. I watered one and ignored the other, and both thrived.

Over the years, many books on plants have been written, but perhaps the first of the really big sellers in this type of writing was one from the early 1970's (I believe) - **THE SECRET LIFE OF PLANTS**. This book tells of the need that ordinary houseplants have for LOVE, for COMPANIONSHIP, how they like certain types of music and how they don't like to have their leaves pulled off. I admit, it seems so weird at first, but after reading a few hundred pages of this stuff, I can see how a person could begin to think seriously about having a conversation with his cactus or bamboo. Many years before THE SECRET LIFE OF PLANTS was ever written, Someone Else was saying things about plants which I think made a lot more sense. JESUS described His message in terms of seeds and plants. Like a good sower, in today's Gospel, Jesus plants His teachings in each of His followers. Within us, God's teachings can either wither and die, or they can live and grow and produce a rich harvest of goodness. That's the clear lesson of the parable in today's Gospel about the sower who sowed the seeds on all different types of soil.

My hunch is that this is a very important parable because it is one of the very few parables that is recorded in 3 out of the 4 Gospels. Matthew, Mark, and Luke all preserve it. And it is just about the only parable that Jesus explained in detail. So I'm guessing it is something God really wants us to know. God gives His teachings and grace to all, but then it's up to us to do something with what God has given us. ANY PLANT WILL DIE IF IT IS NEGLECTED OR IGNORED, AND NOT GIVEN THE PROPER TYPE OF CARE. So too will the Christian Spirit planted in us. The life of Jesus Christ within each one of us will wither and die unless it is nurtured. But like a healthy, growing and cared-for plant, Christ's own life within us will grow and produce a rich harvest of goodness if we tend it with PRAYER, with ATTENTION TO THE WORD OF GOD AT MASS, and with the worthy reception of HOLY COMMUNION. And the nourishing value of just plain old doing good deeds for others should never be overlooked. As Jesus points out elsewhere in His Gospel, even the tiny mustard seed can grow into the largest of plants with a little effort.

The summertime is filled with reminders of growth as we see plants and gardens growing up, and fruits and vegetables being harvested. With a little effort on our part, the Summer of 2008, can also be a time of growth for God's own life within each one of us.

We just need to weed out the roots of evil and nurture the seeds of goodness already planted in our own lives.

We can do it. God can help us if we let Him.

God bless you!

16th Sunday in Ordinary Time - "A"

20 July 2008

FIRST READING: Wisdom 12:13, 16-19
PSALM: Psalm 86:5-6, 9-10, 15-16
SECOND READING: Romans 8:26-27
GOSPEL: Matthew 13:24-43

In the Gospel today, Jesus reminds us that good and evil will exist on the earth until the end of the world, when God will sort it all out.

Before I retired from the Air Force after 29 years of service, I would regularly spend several weeks each summer on an Air Force base. Just before I retired from the military, when I was in my mid-50's, I spent several weeks at Dover Air Force Base in Delaware. The work tempo was really high, and the counseling cases ranged from marriage issues to health issues to deployment issues. But I was really glad to be there supporting the men and women of the United States Air Force.

One new thing that the Air Force introduced that summer was mandatory PT every Monday, Wednesday and Friday. Now PT stands for physical training, and that is definitely not something that I do with any regularity or skill. In fact, when I reported to the gym that summer for my first 90 minutes of mandatory PT, my first comment to the young enlisted airman at the gym entrance counter was **"You know,**

this is the first time I've been in a gym in my adult life!" He laughed and said, **"You mean it's your first time in THIS gym?"** and I told him, **"No, it's my first time in ANY gym."** I looked at all the complicated machines there, and I asked what I could do for the next 90 minutes that wouldn't be harmful to anyone around me or to myself. The trainer suggested that I do some cardio. Do you have any idea how long I had to pedal that stupid bike before it showed that I had lost a measly 200 calories? After that summer, I now have a new respect for what a donut does to me!

And, of course, my age was a continual source of amusement to the young airmen on the base. I still vividly remember when Airman Castenada of the chapel staff (who was just turning 22 years old!) introduced me to a class of newly-enlisted young airmen like this: **"This is Father Charlie. He's a Catholic priest. He's been a priest much longer than I've been alive!"** I smiled as I told the class that if he ever introduced me like that again, Airman Castenada's birth certificate would become a useless document!

It was great ministry. I was glad to be there. And I'm sure I'm going to be telling you a lot more Air Force stories in the months and years ahead of us.

Today's Gospel related Jesus telling the parable of the weeds and the wheat. I'm old enough to know you've heard this one before. But maybe a new story might help us all to understand that the parable really is a good lesson for us that good and bad coexist in our world even today, and that in the end only God is going to sort things out. We're not judges in all this, we're seeds. Our job is to do the best we can to become the wholesome people God wants us to be. Our job is **NOT** to try to do God's job of sorting it all out all the time.

Here's the story.....gleaned from all over the Internet recently.....In the beginning, God created the heavens and the earth, and He populated the earth with BROCCOLI, CAULIFLOWER and SPINACH, green and yellow and red vegetables of all kinds, so man and woman would live long and healthy lives.

Then, using God's great gifts, Satan created Ben & Jerry's ice cream and Krispy Kreme donuts. Satan said: **"You want chocolate with that?"** And man said, **"YES!"** and woman said, **"And as long as you're at it, add some sprinkles!"** And they gained 10 pounds. And Satan smiled.

And God created the healthful yogurt that woman might keep the figure that the man found so fair. and Satan brought forth white flour from the wheat, and sugar from the cane, and combined them into cake! So God said, **"Try my fresh green salad."** and Satan presented THOUSAND-ISLAND DRESSING, BUTTERY CROUTONS, and GARLIC TOAST on the side. And man and woman unfastened their belts.

God then said, **"I have sent you heart-healthy vegetables and olive oil in which to cook them."**

And Satan brought forth deep-fried fish and fried chicken so big it needed its own platter. And man gained more weight and his cholesterol went through the roof.

God then created a light, fluffy white cake and named it **"Angel Food Cake"** and said **"It is good."** Satan then created chocolate cake and named it **"Devil's Food."** God then brought forth running shoes so that His children might lose those extra pounds. And Satan gave us cable TV with a remote control so man would not have to toil changing the channels. And man and woman laughed and cried before the flickering screen and gained many pounds.

Then God brought forth the potato, naturally low in fat and brimming with nutrition. And Satan peeled off the healthful skin and sliced the starchy center into chips and deep-fried them. And man gained more pounds. God then gave lean beef so that man might consume fewer calories and still satisfy his appetite. And Satan created McDonald's and its 99 cent double-cheeseburger. Then he asked, **"Do you want fries with that?"** And man said, **"YES! And super-size them!"** And Satan said, **"It is good."** And man went into cardiac arrest. God sighed and created quadruple bypass surgery. Then Satan created HMO's......and so it goes on until the end of time!

Good and bad coexist in the world event today. And sometimes it is hard to tell them apart. Wheat and weeds still coexist in the world, in this community, and even in the church. But in the end, God will sort things out.

In the meantime, we just need to remember that we're seeds and not judges. And we need to let God be God. God will do the sorting out in the end on His own timetable, not ours. That's the lesson for all of us in today's Gospel. Let God be God, and let Him do the sorting out.

God bless you!

Four views of our beautiful church dedicated in 2003

17th Sunday in Ordinary Time - "A"

27 July 2008

FIRST READING: 1 Kings 3:5, 7-12
PSALM: Psalm 119:57, 72, 76-77, 127-130
SECOND READING: Romans 8:28-30
GOSPEL: Matthew 13:44-52

In the Gospel today, Jesus gives us several beautiful and thoughtful images for His Church in the world.

Well, for me, this is weekend #4 in Laughlin, and it just keeps getting better and better here! A few more buffets, some awesome homemade mushroom soup, fresh ears of corn dropped off by a family, an all-you-can-eat fish dinner.....oh, and I've also enjoyed the Masses and preaching and parishioners and sacraments too! **You sure do know how to make a guy feel welcome here!** I feel like a kid in a candy store with a charge card!

Do you remember an old TV show called "BEYOND BELIEF" on the Sci-Fi Channel? It was an amazing collection of stories that were dramatized and the audience was asked to figure out if the stories really happened or if they were fictional. I loved that show, and I think the key to figuring out some of the stories was to compare them to our own experiences and see if they rang true with what we know of life in our part of the world. That got me thinking about how much we compare things with one another throughout our lives. We do it all the time! When it is very hot outside (as it is sometimes here in Laughlin!), don't we make the comparison and say that it is as **"HOT AS HELL"** here? When we eat a strange food, don't we frequently compare it to a known food by saying something like: **"IT TASTES LIKE CHICKEN"?** I would like to ask your assistance in making some comparisons today here at Mass. We'll do it silently so as not to embarrass anyone. Everyone just think of your own comparisons as we complete these sentences:

1. For me, this whole weekend has been just like a _____.

2. I went to a buffet yesterday and I ate like a _____.

3. Sometimes my son/daughter acts like a _____.

4. Sometimes my husband/wife treats me like a _____.

5. Sometimes my parents make me feel like I'm a _____.

6. God is like a _____.

7. The person sitting next to me today looks like a _____.

Not surprisingly, when Jesus wanted to tell us about His Kingdom, His Church, He used many comparisons. For the past two Sundays, we have heard a whole bunch of these comparisons in the Gospels. Last Sunday, Jesus said that the church is like a **FIELD** in which both **GOOD GRAIN** and **WEEDS** grow together, and like a **MUSTARD SEED which starts**

out very small but grows larger and larger, and like some **YEAST** which is placed in some flour and makes the whole bowl of dough rise.

This weekend, Jesus says that His Church is like a **BURIED TREASURE** which a man finds, and like a **REALLY VALUABLE PEARL** which is worth all of a man's possessions, and like a **HUGE NET** thrown into the sea which collects all sorts of things. **WE USE COMPARISONS WHEN WE SPEAK SO THAT OTHERS WILL BETTER UNDERSTAND WHAT WE THINK AND FEEL AND MEAN. JESUS DOES THE SAME THING. HE WANTS US TO BETTER UNDERSTAND WHAT HE THINKS AND FEELS AND MEANS.**

BECAUSE THE CHURCH is like a **FIELD** with both good grain and weeds, and like a **HUGE NET** with all sorts of things collected in it, we should not be too surprised to discover that church members **(ALL OF US!)** commit sins. **None of us is perfect.....yet!** For now, Jesus wants us to understand that we live in a world where sin and sinners coexist with goodness and saints. Jesus offers us His help because He knows that we need it to sort things out.

BECAUSE THE CHURCH is like a **MUSTARD SEED**, we should realize that it won't always be the center of attention or the largest institution around. It will grow, but growth takes time and effort **(OUR TIME AND OUR EFFORT!)**. Each of us is responsible for some aspect of church growth, maybe by deepening our own knowledge of the Catholic Church and her teachings (when they don't seem to suit our whims and desires), maybe by encouraging or inviting others (even members of our own families) to worship with us. If every family here invited even one other person or family to come to Mass, we'd surely be packed to the rafters! After all, we've found a **TREASURE**, a **PEARL OF GREAT WORTH**. If it is so valuable in our lives, shouldn't we want others, especially our own families and friends, to benefit from it too?

BECAUSE THE CHURCH is like **YEAST** which can make a whole loaf of bread rise, we need to realize that our efforts to uplift those around us are important. The good deeds we do, the kind words we speak, the hurts that we heal, the listening that we do are all **YEAST** for the world, raising it to something higher, something better. And remember.....**NO ACT OF KINDNESS IS EVER TOO SMALL OR TOO INSIGNIFICANT TO BE NOTICED BY GOD.**

No comparison is perfect, but we all can learn something about our Catholic Church and our Christian life from the comparisons Jesus has been giving us these past few summer weekends. And even when it's hot as hell outside, we can be cool as cucumbers inside knowing that we're growing closer to God every day of our lives.

God bless you!

❖ ❖ ❖

18th Sunday in Ordinary Time - "A"

3 August 2008

FIRST READING: Isaiah 55:1-3
PSALM: Psalm 145:8-9, 15-18
SECOND READING: Romans 8:35, 37-39
GOSPEL: Matthew 14:13-21

In the Gospel today, Jesus feeds a crowd of more than 5000 with just a few small fish and a small amount of bread.

Well, here it is, my 5th weekend in Laughlin.....and I still can't decide if I'm on a permanent vacation or if I'm actually working for a living! And the food is so grand! Garlic mashed potatoes, fresh peaches, dried apricots, baked fresh salmon, homemade chicken enchiladas, homemade pineapple upside-down cake and strawberry rhubarb pie have all found their way to me! **Ah, if this is a dream, I hope I never wake up!** By the way, yesterday was National Ice Cream Sandwich Day, and today is National Watermelon Day, so I hope you're going to be celebrating!

A nervous young priest, concluding one of his very first Sunday sermons, told the congregation: "For my text next Sunday, I will take the words from Matthew's Gospel: 'And Jesus fed **FIVE MEN** with **FIVE THOUSAND** loaves of bread and **TWO THOUSAND** fishes.'" A man in the congregation raised his hand and said, "Father, that's not much of a trick. I could do THAT!" The young priest didn't respond, but the next Sunday in the pulpit he repeated his text and this time he did it correctly: **"And Jesus fed FIVE THOUSAND MEN with FIVE loaves and TWO fishes."** Smiling, the young priest said to the man who had questioned him the previous week, **"Could you do that, Mr. Perkins?"** And the man replied, **"I sure could."** **"And how would you do that?"** asked the young priest. And the man responded, **"With all the food that I had left over from last Sunday!"**

I really love today's Gospel about Jesus feeding a crowd of more than 5000 men, not counting the women and children, which probably brought the total number of people fed to be thousands more. I love it because it shows Jesus' care and compassion as well as His awesome power. It is interesting to note that this miracle of feeding the thousands of people with only five barley loaves and two small fish is **ONE OF ONLY TWO** miracles that I know of that are written about in **ALL FOUR** gospels (Matthew, Mark, Luke and John). The other miracle, by the way, is Jesus' Resurrection from the dead! So this is important stuff!

A few thoughts crossed my mind this week about this Gospel and what it teaches us. When we compare ourselves with others , we always run the risk of coming off poorly.

There are always others who look better, speak better, act better, and have more than we do. So we can come away feeling mighty low sometimes.

In today's Gospel, I'm sure that there must have been some people in that crowd who had brought some food with them, probably a lot more than the five loaves and two fish that were offered to Jesus. But it was from such a small beginning that the great miracle of feeding more than 5000 people began.

In many areas of our lives, we might feel that we have only a little to give. We might only have a little money, we might only have a little confidence, we might only have a little time. **The important thing is not so much what we have or even how much we have. The really important thing is to willingly give over what we have to be used by God**. If we had been there that day, would we have shared our five loaves and two fish with Jesus? Or would we have kept them to ourselves figuring that they would never be enough to help in feeding so many thousands of people? **REMEMBER: If that person's lunch had not be given to Jesus, this great miracle might never have happened!**

Think about it this week: God can transform very little into an abundance. I love the part of the story where there are **TWELVE BASKETS** of leftovers gathered up at the end. **God never does "just enough" to get by.** God always gives us **"more than enough"** to meet our needs. And even our small talents, even out little skills, even our small offerings can all be used to accomplish God's great purposes. We just have to be willing to let God use what we have.

God bless you!

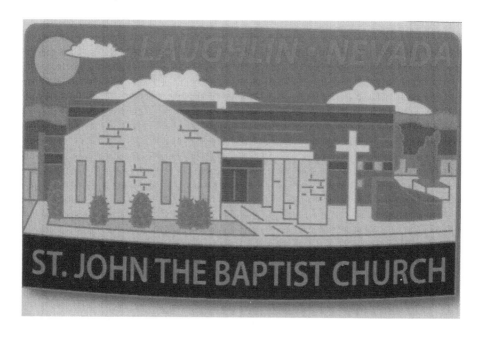

19th Sunday in Ordinary Time - "A"

10 August 2008

FIRST READING: 1 Kings 19:9a, 11-13a
PSALM: Psalm 85:9-14
SECOND READING: Romans 9:1-5
GOSPEL: Matthew 14:22-33

In the Gospel today, Jesus walks on the waters of the sea, terrifying His disciples and yet reminding them of His power.

My 6th weekend in scenic Laughlin, and it just keeps getting better and better! Some weekday mornings, we're getting over 30-35 people for our 8:00 AM Mass, a really beautiful and prayerful group. And the food still keeps coming! Another pineapple upside-down cake, more garlic mashed potatoes, a tuna/macaroni salad with lots of crisp chopped celery, crunchy homemade granola, and a pasta with olive oil and garlic and lots of fresh vegetables. Thank goodness a friend bought me a new belt this week!

I have been accused by some of my friends of making a shameless plea for food and dinner invitations by talking about food in almost every sermon. I have two things to say about that to set the record straight: They're right, and it's working!

Friday of this week, August 15th, is the feast of the Assumption of Mary. It's a holyday of obligation and you can find our Mass schedule in the bulletin. Honoring Mary's Assumption into heaven is a good reminder of our own hope for salvation. Where Mary is now, we hope to be someday.

Of course, here at St. John the Baptist, this is a very special occasion since it marks the 16th anniversary of our Catholic community here in Laughlin. We began on August 15, 1992. we are grateful for the foresight of those men and women who 16 years ago worked to make their dream come true. You and I are here together today because of their hard work and prayers. And I'm really proud to be the 6th priest to serve here as Administrator in our 16 year history. Our celebration this week is a good reminder to us to pray for the priests and people who have come to St. John the Baptist over these past 16 years, and to prepare for those who will be coming in the years ahead. Thanks to the Riverside for their support in giving us this place to worship. **I'm glad to be here at the only church in the Diocese of Las Vegas that has valet parking!** And we thank our local residents and vacationers for your support. We couldn't have done it without you in the past, and we can't do it without you now!

Now that I've reminded you about food and a little bit about our history, we should remember that God has reminders for us too.....and they aren't reminders about feeding the priest! God reminds us constantly that He is thinking of us, that He is with us, and He uses ways that are not always what we would expect.

Consider today's readings.....

ELIJAH expected the Lord in the wind, in the earthquakes, in the fire, **BUT THE LORD CAME TO ELIJAH IN THE TINY WHISPERING BREEZE.**

PAUL expected the life of God to come to him through the Law, through the Prophets, through his observance of the Jewish laws and rituals, **BUT THE LORD JESUS CAME TO HIM AS THE MAN, JESUS CHRIST.**

Jesus' **DISCIPLES** expected a calm sail across the lake, **BUT INSTEAD JESUS CAME WALKING TO THEM ON TOP OF THE WATER.**

There is something basic in our Catholic religion about expecting the unexpected. **GOD COMES TO US IN MANY WAYS, THROUGH MANY PEOPLE, IN MANY SITUATIONS.** Perhaps if we gave it some thought and really looked for it to happen, we wouldn't pass Him by so often when He comes to us at an inconvenient time or in an inappropriate person.

God continues to come to us. Watch for Him, wait for Him. You will not be disappointed. As someone once wisely commented, **"If God had a refrigerator, your picture would be on it."** God wants us to know how much He thinks of us.

God bless you!

✦ ✦ ✦

20th Sunday in Ordinary Time - "A"

17 August 2008

FIRST READING: Isaiah 56:1, 6-7
PSALM: Psalm 67:2-3, 5-6, 8
SECOND READING: Romans 11:13-15, 29-32
GOSPEL: Matthew 15:21-28

In the Gospel today, Jesus gives us the example of the Canaanite woman whose prayer was persistent and honest.

Chopped apples, almonds, walnuts, marshmallows, cream.....I'm just guessing but I think these were some of the ingredients in an awesome Waldorf Salad that I was given this week! And then there were a few bags of homemade oatmeal/raison cookies. I tell you, this has been a great week! I even got up to Vegas to see some of my friends. And whenever I ask why they haven't come to Laughlin, they always whine about it being **"too hot"** and **"so far away."** Hey, I do the drive in just over an hour and 20 minutes.....that's not far! And besides, we beat Vegas in the heat any day! After all, we've got a river, all they have is heat! I'm thinking of signing up with the Laughlin Visitors Center to promote the joy of being in Laughlin!

Many years ago in the State of Illinois, a young man with six months of schooling to his credit ran for an office in the legislature. As might be expected, he was badly beaten. Next he entered business, but failed in that too, and he spent most of the next 17 years paying the debts that his worthless partner had accumulated. He suffered a nervous break-down. He ran for Congress and was defeated. He then tried to obtain an appointment to the U.S. Land Office, but didn't succeed. He became a candidate for Vice President of the United States, and lost. Two years later, he was defeated in a race for the United States Senate. Later, he ran for President and finally was elected. **That man was Abraham Lincoln.**

It took Sir Winston Churchill **THREE** years to get through the British equivalent of 8th grade because he couldn't pass the **ENGLISH** exam. But in 1941, as Britain's Prime Minister, he gave a famous wartime speech to a class of school children in which he said: **"NEVER EVER GIVE UP!"** Just like Abraham Lincoln, he knew the importance of persistence!

In today's Gospel, the Canaanite woman repeatedly asks Jesus to grant her request. **She never gives up!** And I think we can learn two important characteristics of prayer from this event: **Prayer should be persistent and prayer should be humble.**

God is not our servant, a genie who comes out of the bottle at our beck and call. God is the Almighty Creator of the Universe Who in His infinite goodness chooses to listen to us as His children. We do not have a right to His gifts or to His interest. God's gifts and God's interest are given to us because of His goodness. In other words, God hears us when we pray **NOT BECAUSE WE ARE GOOD, BUT BECAUSE HE IS GOOD.** It takes a humble person to accept this.

And when we pray, we present ourselves before God knowing that He will hear us, and that He will respond to us in the way and at the time He chooses. Prayer doesn't change God, but persistent and humble prayer can change us so that we can be ready to receive whatever God wants to do for us.

Did you ever wonder why the priest usually prays with his hands out like this? Try it with me.....just put your hands out, palms facing up. Doesn't it look like we're ready to receive and accept whatever God wants to give? That's pretty much what we're doing when we pray.

It's a hot summer weekend. There's no need for a long sermon. The message is clear.....when we pray, never give up. God will do His part because God is good. And that's really good for us.

God bless you!

21st Sunday in Ordinary Time - "A"

24 August 2008

FIRST READING: Isaiah 22:19-23
PSALM: Psalm 138:1-3, 6-8
SECOND READING: Romans 11:33-36
GOSPEL: Matthew 16:13-20

In the Gospel today, Jesus challenges us to answer the question He once posed to His disciples: "Who do you say that I am?"

Ah, the joys of living in Laughlin continue! A spicy chicken fiesta soup, delicious egg salad rollups, cinnamon nut rolls, peach cobbler, tuna casserole, German chocolate cake, some wonderful pasta.....the list goes on and on. But the joys of living in Laughlin are not only good eats: no, there's more to it than that. This week I knew I needed a haircut. I've been driving up to Nellis Air Force Base in Vegas for haircuts since I've been here. But I have decided that I need a barber locally. Now I always insist that my doctor, my dentist, my lawyer and my barber have to be younger than I am. I hate changing them, so I need them to outlive me. Well, I was walking through the Laughlin Town Center on Tuesday and saw a sign on a barber/beauty shop which read: "Walk-Ins Welcome" so I went in. I told the woman that I wanted a military haircut, short all over, white walls on the ears, and a really clean neck. After she finished the haircut, she said,

"Come with me." And I said "Where?" She told me that a shampoo comes with each haircut. So she had me settle into this really comfortable chair and let my head hang back into a sink. I told her no one had ever done this to my hair before! But when she put the shampoo in and started rubbing my temples, I felt so contented, with that giddy look that a dog gets when you're rubbing his head! At first, I was worried because I realized that I hadn't asked her how much this haircut would cost, but it felt so good that I decided I really didn't care what it would cost! Whatever the cost, it would be worth it! It was absolutely refreshing, and the whole thing cost a lot less than a simple haircut back in New Jersey. No wonder people drive hundreds of miles to get to Laughlin! Golly, I'm glad to be living here! I might be needing a haircut every week now!

During an interview some years ago, I heard that a famous TV host had been asked, **"If you could interview anyone in history, who would it be?"** And the TV host replied instantly that it would be **"Jesus of Nazareth."** Then he was asked, **"If you could ask Him just one question, what would it be?"** After a brief pause, he responded, **"I think I would like to ask Him, were You truly virgin born?. Because if He was, that would change everything."** I guess we might all like to ask Jesus a question like that. If Jesus truly is Who the Gospels say He is - Our God and Our Savior , born of the Virgin Mary - then all that He said about life and death, sin and salvation, God and the devil, heaven and hell would be true.

That TV host is right! If Jesus is Our God and Our Savior, that would change everything. Do you think we'd be careless about coming to church each week if we really believed God is here? Do you think we'd have our children baptized, but then never bring them to church if we really believed in Jesus? Do you think we'd send our kids to religious education classes and then never make it a family priority to come to church on Sunday if we really believed in Jesus? **If we really believed, then our actions would show it.** We would try to follow what Jesus taught and what His Catholic Church teaches because Jesus really is our God and our Savior.

One Sunday morning, a man showed up in church with both of his ears terribly burned and blistered. So his pastor asked, **"Jim, what happened to you?"** He replied, **"I was lying on the couch watching a ball game on TV while my wife was ironing nearby. I was totally engrossed in the game when she went out of the room, leaving the iron near the phone. The phone rang, and keeping my eyes on the TV, I grabbed the hot iron and put it up to my ear."** "That's awful," gasped the pastor, **"but how did the other ear get burned?"** Jim said, **"Well, you see, no sooner did I hang up, and the guy called back again!"** Jim just didn't get it! Lots of folks never seem to get it and never seem to understand how life really works, even at the simplest levels. That's why Jesus is pressing His followers, and us, with a challenging question in today's Gospel - **"Who do you say that I am?"**

And Jesus takes us even further along the path of being His disciples by reminding us that it's one thing to say the right words, but it's something else to live them out each day, each month, each year. In today's Gospel, the disciples knew how to say the right words - "You are the Christ!", but when it came to understanding what that belief would cost them - the self-denial, the suffering, the reality of giving their whole lives over to the Lord - they just didn't have a clue. They just didn't get it! And Jesus had to explain one more time that being His follower wasn't always going to be easy. Sometimes the disciples would be hurt because they had to choose to do what was right, not what was convenient.

Jesus doesn't want to know what other people think or do, He is asking each one of us directly, "Who do YOU say that I am?" And if we really know WHO Jesus is, then that means that our lives will be different. Just as Peter's life, and the lives of the Apostles, were different because of WHO Jesus is.

If Jesus is Our God and Our Savior as we say He is, then shouldn't He have some control over our actions and over our lives? For those of us who come on Sunday, what we say here is great, but what we do the rest of the week is just as significant. **If our actions on Monday match our words on Sunday, fine; if not, we need to make some changes.**

God bless you!

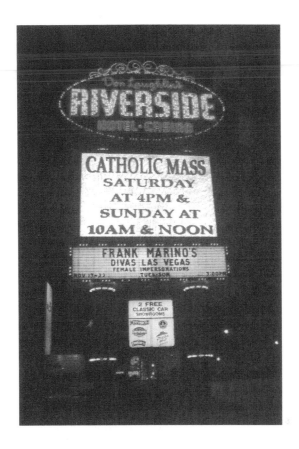

Yes, we even make it on the Riverside Sign each weekend!

22nd Sunday in Ordinary Time - "A"

31 August 2008

FIRST READING: Jeremiah 20:7-9
PSALM: Psalm 63:2-6, 8-9
SECOND READING: Romans 12:1-2
GOSPEL: Matthew 16:21-27

In the Gospel today, Jesus reminds us that following Him always involves the cross as well as the resurrection.

Ah, Labor Day weekend in Laughlin.....unfortunately accompanied by some New Jersey-like weather! Hopefully, it will clear for Monday. I just hope I didn't bring it with me from New Jersey when I moved here.

Well, the Laughlin Report is still awesome! Brownies and parsley potatoes, corn on the cob, a couple of buffets. And now I have discovered that there are **GREAT LOCALS' DISCOUNTS** for meals and shows at the Laughlin casinos. It just keeps getting better and better here!

On Friday night, I came to the **GOOD VIBRATIONS** show at the Riverside. That's when I discovered the **GREAT LOCALS' DISCOUNTS!** They cut the show price in half! I loved the Beach Boys when I was growing up in the 1960's, and now just hearing their music again when I'm in my 60's was awesome! Even the song titles brought back super memories: **HELP ME**

RHONDA, LITTLE DEUCE COUPE, CALIFORNIA GIRLS, 409, BARBARA ANN, BE TRUE TO YOUR SCHOOL, SURFIN' USA, SLOOP JOHN B, and so many more! I actually closed my eyes during some of the songs and I was 17 and back at a high school dance in New Jersey with my girlfriend! (Don't worry.....she got married, has two kids and is a grandmother now!) It is amazing how music can bring back so many great memories.

Speaking of memories, whenever I read today's Gospel, I always think of a story I heard many years ago.

A young wife was in the mall and she passed a store window and saw a beautiful red dress. Money was tight so she just looked at it and continued walking. But it stayed in her mind and she came back to the store window again, and again. Finally she went in, tried the dress on, and bought it. When she got home, she showed it to her husband who was less than thrilled at the expense. He asked her, "Don't you remember the line from Sunday's Gospel - **'GET THEE BEHIND ME, SATAN?'** You should have thought of that when you were tempted to buy that dress." The wife looked at him and said, "Of course I remembered the line from Sunday's Gospel! And, of course, I knew I was being tempted to buy that dress. So I did say **"GET THEE BEHIND ME, SATAN"** But then Satan said, **"SURE LOOKS GREAT FROM THE BACK TOO!"**

Temptation is an interesting part of life. We may know right from wrong, but it's still pretty easy to be tempted. As many of us realize, life isn't always an easy romp through the park. It has its difficult moments. And that can be jarring to us because we can sometimes think that because we try to be good, there should be no difficulties in our lives. And that's just not what happens in real life.

Like Peter in today's Gospel, we sometimes feel much more comfortable with a Christianity that doesn't include the cross. If we try to be good, we figure that there should be no suffering in our lives. Today's readings bring us sharply back to reality. There will be sacrifices and crosses to bear, the ways and standards of the world are not necessarily the ways and standards of God, and to walk in the footsteps of Jesus Christ means at times to be carrying a cross. Jesus leaves no doubt.....it can be difficult to do what is right and to avoid what is wrong.

We don't like difficulty or hardship. And even though God doesn't promise to remove them from our lives, He does promise something even more powerful - God promises to accompany us on our journey through life. **No matter what happens, God promises that we won't have to face it all alone.** We need to remember that!

Labor Day Weekend brings an unofficial end of summer and a reminder that our normal patterns of life are resuming. May the days and weeks ahead of us bring us closer to God, and may we all feel His power and His presence in whatever life may bring.

Yes, there will be joys; and, yes, there will be difficulties. **But God will be with us through all of them.** As we worship God today here at Mass, we renew our commitment to Him, we acknowledge our dependence upon Him, and we thank Him for accompanying us on our journey through life.

If might be a good idea to spend a little time thinking back on our lives this week - the good times and the hard times - and reflect a bit on how God really has been with us through it all. The good times are better because of God, and the hard times are endurable because of God. And never forget that **GOD IS WITH US THOUGH ALL OF THE TIMES OF OUR LIVES.** That's even better than remembering the words of a Beach Boys' song!

God bless you!

23rd Sunday in Ordinary Time - "A"

7 September 2008

FIRST READING: Ezekiel 33:7-9
PSALM: Psalm 95:1-2, 6-9
SECOND READING: Romans 13:8-10
GOSPEL: Matthew 18:15-20

In the Gospel today, Jesus reminds us that He will always be with us, that where two or three gather in His name, He will be present with them.

The Laughlin Report for this week continues to be **exceptional!** Within the past few days, I've received a box of cinnabons, pistachio ice cream, chocolate cookies, homemade potato salad with radishes and onions, an au-gratin potato casserole, homemade white jello with fruit, homemade tuna salad, fresh grapes, and some really awesome jalapeno bagels! (I never even knew anyone sold jalapeno bagels!) And I found out that there is no coroner here in Laughlin, so if I die in Laughlin, by law, they have to take my body to Las Vegas! **How cool is that? Even when I'm dead, I'll get to go to Vegas!** I tell you, it just keeps getting better and better here!

I have to admit that I don't want to tell the other priests in the diocese about this place. They'd all be fighting to get sent here! So it will just be our little secret!

When I was first ordained as a priest, and I wanted to remind people of the importance of certain pivotal events in our history, I would ask the question - **"What were you doing when you heard that President Kennedy had been shot?"** And everyone remembered where he/she was at that moment in history. Later on, when I was teaching high school, I changed the question to - **"What were you doing when you heard about the Challenger exploding?"** Obviously, in the wake of the events of 2001, my question has now changed to - **"What were you doing when the planes hit the World Trade Center?"**

The point is that there are events in the life of our world that make an undeniable impact on it, that are literally **unforgettable**. And sometimes we can be so caught up with these events that we forget to keep them in perspective. As terrible as the Islamic terrorist attack on the USA was on September 11, 2001, it **was not** and **is not** the only focus of our lives. Life goes on even in the face of life-changing events. So, it might be good for us to be reminded of some of the other important things that make up our lives.

We all know that there was a big religious fervor that gripped our nation following 9/11/01. For several weeks, our churches were filled to overflowing. But people have very short memories, and the unchurched quickly went back to their old habits. Fortunately, the faithful who were in church on the week before September 11th continued their old habits too. I'm sure we might see a touch of that same dynamic following any disaster. But what is our responsibility to those who only come to worship when they feel desperate? Today's First Reading says that we need to be **"watchmen"**, looking out for them, calling them back to the right ways of thinking and acting. **As faithful Catholics, we are in some real way responsible for one another.** And this applies not only to parents who need to teach their children by word and example the importance of practicing our Catholic Faith, but it also applies to all of us. We need to be alert to praising what is good in our families and in our communities. But we also need to be alert to any signs of evil and not be afraid to stand up for what is right, and what is true, and what is good. In a very real way, we show our love for God by the love we show to those around us.

This week, consider your role as "**watchmen**", as people who are committed to not only bringing yourselves to God, but also encouraging others to come to Him also. Be aware of all the good around you, and **encourage** it to continue by your words, by your actions, and by your support. Be aware too of any signs of evil or neglect and be sure to **discourage** evil by your words, by your actions and by your support for evil to be eliminated. This is how we all work to fulfill the law of love for our God and for our neighbor.

I strongly encourage all of you to pray to God on Thursday of this week as we remember the 7th Anniversary of 9/11/01. Yes, 9/11/01 was an unforgettable event in our personal and national history. But our Catholic Faith and our hope and our concern for one another go on into the future. And in today's Gospel, God promises to be with us as we gather. There is great power in the ending of today's Gospel as Jesus tells us: **"For where two or three are gathered together in My Name, there am I in the midst of them."** Never forget that God promises to be with us whenever we pray together.

If you want to be where God is, you're in the right place right where you are!

God bless you!

The Exaltation of the Holy Cross

14 September 2008

FIRST READING: Numbers 21:4b-9
PSALM: Psalm 78:1b-2, 34-38
SECOND READING: Philippians 2:6-11
GOSPEL: John 3:13-17

In the Gospel today, Jesus reminds us that God loves us, and wants to save us so we can share eternity with Him.

The Laughlin Report this week is exceptional..... even by my high expectations! Homemade cheese enchiladas, homemade fresh salsa, homemade cream of tomato soup, homemade cream of asparagus soup, barbecued chicken made according to an old Alabama family recipe, and so much more! I don't think I'm going to have my cholesterol checked for the whole time I'm assigned here!

I went to my first Laughlin Chamber of Commerce mixer on Thursday. It was a great meeting with so many of the community leaders there. And wouldn't you know, they had a great buffet dinner! And then, they had a 50/50 raffle. As soon as I bought my tickets, I said to the folks at my table, **"I'm going to win this!"** And I did! So now I'm $90.00 richer.

And I didn't even have to go to Vegas for my magic shows this week! Got to see magical entertainer Aaron Radatz right here at the Riverside on Thursday night, and I'm going again tonight! And maybe again on Sunday night! Awesome show! The magic comes right here to me! And there's even a 2 for 1 deal for locals! **I love this place!**

And this week Laughlin just rolled out a new tourism slogan through a paid professional advertising agency. It's kind of catchy: **"Laughlin: It's like you own the place!"** I wish they would have consulted me first.....my suggestion would have been: **"Laughlin: It just keeps getting better and better!"** I feel so comfortable here!

Today's Feast of the Exaltation of the Holy Cross might make us feel uncomfortable. I don't think many of us like the cross. I think we all feel uncomfortable thinking about the fact that Jesus suffered and died a horrible death on a wooden cross on a hill in Israel. Of all the unusual situations that have occurred in this world, certainly the death of Jesus Christ, the Son of God, on the cross ranks as one of the most uniquely unusual. It had never happened before and it has never happened again. It is a pivotal and unique event in the history of the world. And I think that thinking about it sometimes bothers some of us. It's hard to think about God suffering and dying.

I did a little research into today's Feast of the Exaltation of the Holy Cross. It commemorates the finding of the true cross on which Jesus died by St. Helena in 322, and the dedication of a church on that site in 335 on this date, September 14th.

The year is 322. The world is enjoying a period of relative peace. Constantine, the first Roman emperor to embrace Christianity, had issued the Edict of Milan a decade earlier. After centuries of persecution, Christians are now free to practice their Faith openly. Churches are being built and people begin to want to seek out their Christian roots. Constantine's mother, Helena, had become a Christian, which probably definitely influenced her son to stop the persecutions even before he became a Christian! Mothers have a lot of power! And now Helena has decided that she wants to make a journey to Jerusalem to see for herself the places where Jesus lived and taught and suffered and died. Of course, having a son who is the emperor of the whole Roman Empire, helped to make this journey possible.

So Helena journeys to Jerusalem and according to a legend finds the wood of three crosses buried on the hill that we know as Calvary. Could one of these three crosses be the actual cross of Jesus? The bishop of Jerusalem suggests a test. And a dying woman is brought in. One by one she touches each of the three crosses. The third one brought about a miraculous cure. Helena had discovered the true cross. On this date in the year 335, the church of the Holy Sepulchre was dedicated on the site of Calvary.

The cross is a powerful symbol of our Catholic Christian Faith. We begin and end our prayers by making the Sign of the Cross, we mark a cross on our foreheads, lips and hearts before the Gospel is read (Just in passing, that gesture is made by the priest with the words, **"May the Lord be on my mind, on my lips and in my heart that I may worthily and fittingly proclaim His Holy Gospel."** Over the years, the Faithful have wordlessly imitated that action praying that God would be in their minds, on their lips, and in their hearts as well.) In giving a blessing, the Sign of the Cross is made over the person or the object to be blessed.

And of course, our churches always contain many artistic representations of the cross. What once was an instrument of torture and shame has become for us an emblem of value and pride. It is a solemn and powerful reminder of the truth of today's Gospel, John 3:16: **"For God so loved the world that He gave His only Son, so that he who believes in Him might not perish, but might have eternal life."**

What could make us uncomfortable really should give us the greatest comfort. The cross is a constant reminder to all of us of how very much God loves us. Every time we make the Sign of the Cross, we remind ourselves that we are loved by God and that we belong to God. And that's the best good news of all!

God bless you!

A powerful set of images drawn by Father Charlie's friend Christopher Doane. It hangs proudly in Father Charlie's office.

25th Sunday in Ordinary Time - "A"

21 September 2008

FIRST READING: Isaiah 55:6-9
PSALM: Psalm 145:2-3, 8-9, 17-18
SECOND READING: Philippians 1:20c-24, 27a
GOSPEL: Matthew 20:1-16a

In the Gospel today, Jesus teaches us the importance of perspective. A lot depends on where we see ourselves in His parables.

What a week! Last Sunday night, I was invited backstage by Aaron Radatz, the magician doing the show at the Riverside. So I got to watch the whole magic show from behind the scenes, meet all the cast members, and learn how it all worked. For a magic fan like me, it was better than meeting the pope! **Really...better than meeting the pope!** Oh, I can't tell you any of the secrets I learned. If I told you, I would have to kill you.....or something like that!

And the awesome foods this week included a Boston creme cake, homemade brownies and strawberry shortcake, homemade rice pudding, and an apple crisp from a parishioner who said she wanted to be sure she got on my list for Sunday!

And on Thursday, I was up in Vegas for a meeting of the priests in the seven parishes that make up our vicariate. I liked meeting the other guys who felt sorry for me being so far away from Vegas! They just haven't got a clue as to how awesome life is here on the river! And then they served lunch at the meeting which ended with some peanut butter cookies and Greek baklava. The joys of being here in Laughlin just never end.

Today I'd like to talk about perspective.....Things really do look different depending on your vantage point. Every now and then, a child comes out of Mass when I'm standing outside the church and hands me a pencil or crayon drawing that he has made for me during Mass. Sometimes the drawings are really easy to understand; sometimes I have to look really hard to see what the drawing shows. If I were an art critic, I may not see much in these drawings, frequently done on the backs of church bulletins or on scraps of paper. But as a priest, these are works of real art. They speak volumes to me of the child's interest in religion, and the child's trust that something as personal as his artwork could be shared with me. It's at times like this that I feel most like a parent, and that's a good feeling.

I think the same is true in much of our lives. Our perspective colors everything. I happened to attend a talk once about investment strategies. But it turned out to be a talk about investment strategies for those with $100,000 or more to invest. It was an interesting talk, but my big issue wasn't how to invest $100,000; my big issue was how to get the $100,000 in the first place!

When I was a teacher at St. Joe's High School, I once ended up with a sophomore who was the son of a high school classmate of mine. When his father (my classmate) came in for parent/teacher night, he asked me how his son was doing in my class. I told the father that his son was misbehaving, acting like the class clown, and not really keen on doing any homework at all. In fact, I said, he's just like you were when we were in class together. It was funny when I was your classmate; it's not funny anymore when I'm the teacher.

Even in the spiritual life, perspective is important. St. Ignatius Loyola tells us in his writings that when we read a biblical parable, we need to see where we stand inside the parable. In other words, we need to judge what our perspective is. This will help us to understand better the parable Jesus is telling.

Today's Gospel is a great example of the importance of perspective. The parable is about a wealthy landowner who hires laborers at various times during the day, and then at the end of the day, the landowner calls in his foreman and tells him to pay each of the laborers the exact same wage no matter how long he has worked. So those who worked a full day get the same pay as those who have worked for only an hour.

Many people listen to that parable even today and their first reaction is **"That's not fair!"**..."**What is that landowner thinking**"...**If I worked a full day, I should get more than that other person who only worked**

for an hour!" You can fill in your own reactions. **Do you know why we think that way?** Because you and I automatically assume that **WE** are the ones who have worked the full day in that parable. It's a matter of perspective. Suppose just for an instant that we **REALLY** are the ones who haven't worked very long or very hard. We just happened to be in the right place at the right time, and happened to be hired by this really generous landowner. How would we react to getting the full day's pay for only an hour of work? **We'd be bouncing off the walls with sheer excitement and happiness!** We'd be thinking how fortunate we are. We'd probably be really grateful to the landowner, and maybe even to God for our good fortune! It's all a matter of our perspective.

Our Catholic Faith tells us that grace and the opportunity to share life with God as Catholic Christians in this life and the hope for eternal life with God in heaven is **NOT** payment for what we are owed by God. It is rather a free and generous gift from God to us, not because we are so good, but because **GOD IS SO GOOD!**

If you think about this parable from this different perspective, I suggest that you will come away with a deep sense of gratitude. We're the lucky ones. We're the ones who have gotten so much more than we ever could have deserved. It's all a matter of perspective.

God bless you!

Some of the beautiful Laughlin scenery, including the magnificent Colorado River.

26th Sunday in Ordinary Time - "A"

28 September 2008

FIRST READING: Ezekiel 18:25-28
PSALM: Psalm 25:4-9
SECOND READING: Philippians 2:1-11
GOSPEL: Matthew 21:28-32

In the Gospel today, Jesus presents us with the story of two very different sons. I think we've met people very much like them in the course of our lives.

Some people have been telling me that for some reason they find they are always leaving Mass feeling hungry! Me too! Don't know why that is! The Laughlin experience continues to get better and better. This week I got invited out to a great seafood buffet.....and it was only lunchtime! And then there was a chicken casserole, and a pork and sauerkraut casserole, and then carrot muffins and lemon poppy seed muffins, and then some apple coffee cake. **I am, however, managing to get into shape here. The only problem is that the shape is ROUND!**

And this week, all my stuff arrived from New Jersey on a 53 foot long tractor trailer. And we off-loaded it all to the storage center on Needles Highway. So now I have about 500 boxes to unpack! That will be fun as I go through what I've accumulated over the past 60 years of my life! I think there will be a big garage sale someday! And the truck driver was this really cool guy named DJ from Shreveport, Louisiana. He was built like a tank, with hands that could palm a basketball. He saw how awed I was by his truck, so he asked me if I had ever ridden in one. I said, "No." So he said, "Hop in, and let's go for a ride!" I felt like a little kid climbing into that truck! I've wanted to do that all my life! I told him that if he ever passes near Laughlin again, I wanted to take him out to dinner to thank him. He said he'd really like that a lot because I was real easy to talk to. But he also said that he couldn't let me pay for the dinner. He said he would only go to dinner with me if he paid for it. I asked him why I couldn't pay, and he told me that back in Louisiana he was always taught to be good to his elders!

Of all the things that I get to do as a priest, one of the things I like best is officiating at weddings. There is something so beautiful about being asked to be the priest at a wedding for a couple. I've married hundreds of couples in my years as a priest, and no two weddings ever seem to be the same. **They are certainly never boring to me!** Something interesting always seems to happen. Like the best man forgetting the rings, or the church catching on fire during the wedding ceremony, or the video cameraman rolling his video cart up on the train of the bride's gown, or the maid of honor (the bride's sister) who attempted to fix the bride's dress during the opening prayer, stepped on the veil, tried to balance herself, slipped on the hem of her own gown, grabbed the bouquet of flowers on the altar rail and broke the vase. Not to scare off any prospective brides and grooms, but if I had a video camera with me at the weddings I have done, I could have made a fortune selling my tapes to America's Funniest Home Videos!

But as unpredictable as the weddings themselves are (and everything I have just described has really happened at a wedding that I officiated at), the wedding rehearsal dinners are even more fun. That's when I gather information. I've discovered that after a few beers or glasses of wine, people will tell a priest anything. They think I'd never repeat it!

I thought of what I have learned about couples at their wedding rehearsal dinners as I read over today's Gospel. I'll bet I could have found out a lot about those two sons if I had gone to their wedding rehearsal dinners! I'll bet their friends and family could have told me some stories, could have clued me in on what those two guys were really like.

The **FIRST SON** would promise you anything, but when it came down to the wire, he wouldn't deliver. He'd find some excuse, or he'd have gotten a better offer elsewhere. "I forgot"......"I was too busy"......"Something came up"......."I really wanted to help, but I had other things to do." He was all talk and no action. I think we all know people like that. They talk a good game, but they never show up to do the work.

The **OTHER SON** was different. He might not sound really loyal or really helpful, but he certainly knew where his loyalties were, and where his help was needed. When the time came for work to be done, he'd be there working. I'll bet his friends and family could tell me some great stories about how this some had come through for them when they really needed him. He might not have been much on saying nice things, but he didn't let you down when you needed help. I think we all know people like him, people who are always there, working without calling attention to themselves, doing what has to be done. Pastors love people like that!

Wedding rehearsal dinners remind me that sometimes it is good to step back and think how other people see us. Are we just **TALKERS** or are we really **DOERS**? Whether it concerns helping the poor by donating our money, spending some of our valuable time listening to a friend who needs to talk, or just keeping our commitments to our family, to our friends, to our parish and our community, or whether it concerns breaking a bad habit like smoking or eating or drinking too much, or forming a good habit like praying more frequently or getting to Mass on time, are we mere **TALKERS** or are we really **DOERS**?

Or to put it another way, if I were doing your wedding tomorrow, what would your family and friends be telling me about you at the rehearsal dinner tonight? It's something to think about, and it might be something to do something about too!

God bless you!

Father Charlie (center) enjoying a day off with Michael, Eddie, Charlie and Paul.

27th Sunday in Ordinary Time - "A"

5 October 2008

FIRST READING: Isaiah 5:1-7
PSALM: Psalm 80: 9, 12-16, 19-20
SECOND READING: Philippians 4:6-9
GOSPEL: Matthew 21:33-43

In the Gospel today, Jesus reminds us that God wants to have a wonderful relationship with us, but we need to be compliant.

The Laughlin Report continues to be spectacular! And it's not just the food which by the way included apple spice muffins, a surprise gift of cinnamon rolls left in the fridge at the rectory, tuna salad with peas, and a promise of homemade peanut brittle in the coming weeks! After last week's mention of how happy I was to get a ride on the 18 wheeler, one of our parishioners asked if I would like to go out on a jet ski on the river. I told him there was a big difference between riding an 18 wheeler and riding a jet ski! For one, I always WANTED to ride on an 18 wheeler! I've never thought about riding on jet ski! And when he asked me if I had a Speedo to wear, I knew it would be a problem! I think there's a state or federal law against making a Speedo in my size (or at least against WEARING a Speedo in my size!).

And I've been looking for a backscratcher for several weeks. I don't want one of those stubby wooden ones! I want one with the sharp fingers of a hand on the end of it. I stopped in one of the local stores and asked if they had one. The saleslady said, "Sure", but then brought over one of the stubby wooden ones. However, she wanted to make a sale so the saleslady started scratching my back with it., Ah, the joys of living in Laughlin! By the way, I was talking about this earlier in the week in the church office and so far I have received FIVE backscratchers! I've got to be careful about mentioning things I want around here!

Today is the annual observance of RESPECT LIFE SUNDAY in our Catholic Church as we begin the month of October which is RESPECT LIFE MONTH. Yesterday was the Feast Day of St. Francis of Assisi. St. Francis serves as a great reminder of our responsibilities towards this world and everyone and everything in it. If ever there was anyone who loved and respected all life, it was St. Francis. He knew what was important in life. He knew that life itself was beautiful and wonderful - an incredible gift from God - something to be appreciated and gratefully cared for. He lived each day to the fullest, and he knew he was always in the presence of God. He knew the peace of God of which today's Second Reading speaks so eloquently. He seemed to radiate so much of God's love and peace that he brought a sense of peace with him wherever he went. Some of the ancient legends about St. Francis even tell us that the animals listened to him when he preached. He was at peace with all nature. He loved life and respected all forms of life - human, animal, plant. He loved nature and was probably the first true ecologist. And he knew how to laugh. He never took himself too seriously. We have a lot to learn from St. Francis about a healthy and happy approach to life. There is more good than evil in the world, and St. Francis always knew how to find it. We need to see the world with the eyes of St. Francis.

So today we pray that like St. Francis we all might feel God's abiding presence and learn to treat all life with respect because all life comes from God. We show respect for life in so many varied ways. If we drive, we should drive carefully. If we speak, we should speak truthfully. If we work, we should work honestly. From the moment of conception to the moment of natural death, we owe it all to God. And we owe it all to one another to cherish and respect the life and the lives that God has entrusted to us.

Some years ago, when I was visiting Laughlin, I told a story about a duck, and everyone seemed to like it and remember it. So I've found another story about a duck, and I think it fits in well for today. It's called **"GRANDMOTHER'S DUCK."**

A little boy visiting his grandparents was given a slingshot. He practiced often in the woods, but he never hit his target. One day as he returned to Grandma's backyard, he spied her pet duck. On an impulse, he took aim and let a stone fly. The stone hit, and the duck fell down dead. The boy panicked. In desperation, he hid the dead duck in the woodpile. When he looked up, he saw his sister Sally watching. **She had seen it all, but she said nothing.** After lunch that day, Grandma said, "Sally, let's wash the dishes." But Sally said, "Johnny told me he wanted to help in the kitchen today. Didn't you, Johnny?" And she whispered to him, **"Remember the duck!"** So Johnny did the dishes. Later Grandpa asked if the children wanted to go fishing. Grandma said, "I'm sorry, but I need Sally to help me make supper." Sally smiled and said, "That's all taken care of. Johnny wants to do it." Again she whispered, **"Remember the duck!"** So Johnny stayed while Sally went fishing with Grandpa. After several days of Johnny doing both his own chores and all of Sally's chores, finally he couldn't stand it anymore. He went to Grandma and confessed that he hadn't meant to do it, but he'd killed her pet duck. "I know, Johnny," Grandma said. She gave him a hug. "I was standing at the window and saw the whole thing. Because I love you, I already forgave you. I just wondered how long you would let Sally make a slave out of you."

How long? That's the question raised by Jesus by telling the parable of the wicked tenants in today's Gospel. Jesus reminds us of the blessings showered upon us in life and the consequences of our disobedience. He warns us that we must "pay the rent" instead of rebelling against God and refusing His word. Both the first reading from Isaiah and the parable in the Gospel tell us how much God loves us and wants a relationship with us. The choice is now ours: rebellion or relationship? God already loves us and forgives us. He just wants us to do our part in returning to Him when we stray, and in not letting our past sins enslave us, and in trying to see all life as God sees it.

As you leave Mass today, I hope you'll take one or several of these little cards from me as a reminder to see and add kindness to life in the coming weeks of this Respect Life Month. It's part of an "Experiment in Anonymous Kindness." The idea is that you do something nice for someone else, then leave this little card behind to spread it around. If you would like some suggestions of nice things to do, they even provide a list which I'm leaving at our gift shop tables.

Over 1000 people will attend our Masses this weekend. Just imagine what could happen this week if we all did just one random act of kindness in our home towns. Now that's how to really celebrate Respect Life Month!

God bless you!

28th Sunday in Ordinary Time - "A"

12 October 2008

FIRST READING: Isaiah 25:6-10a
PSALM: Psalm23:1-6
SECOND READING: Philippians 4:12-14, 19-20
GOSPEL: Matthew 22:1-14

In the Gospel today, Jesus invites us to the banquet with God in eternity and exposes the weaknesses of our flimsy excuses.

I got a letter from a priest/friend of mine in New York this week. He got a new assignment at the same time I came out here to Laughlin. His letter begins with: "I hate my job! Just another 45 months and I'll be out of it!" I almost felt guilty for the letter I had sent him telling him how much I love Laughlin!

And this week has been another awesome one in Laughlin! There were garlic mashed potatoes, cheesecake, oatmeal-raison cookies and a chocolate cruller, homemade chow mein, and some grapes to be healthy. And homemade peanut brittle that melts in your mouth! I got to see Jeff McBride's MAGIC ON THE EDGE show in Las Vegas on my day off, and got to hang out with another magician during the day. Decided to gamble a little, so I put $20 into my Mom's slot machine in Vegas (it's a Wheel of Fortune machine, and the number on it is 1912, the year my Mom was born, and it always pays off for me!). In just 8 spins, I turned my $20 into over $500! **Thanks, Mom!**

This has nothing to do with the sermon, but I have to tell you that the last line in today's Gospel brings me back to my high school days. "Many are called, but few are chosen." I had to give a talk in English class selling an item with a reference to literature, so I chose to sell "Matthew's Radiators." They were produced by a small company in Palestine at the time of Jesus, but never seemed to provide enough heat. So their slogan was taken right from today's Gospel: **"Many are cold, but few are frozen."** ...... Sorry, but I've waited for years to use that!

Now, back to the sermon.....

To make it possible for everyone to attend church next Sunday as they should, we are going to have a special "No Excuse" Sunday.

Cots will be placed in the aisles for those who say "But Sunday is my only day to sleep."

We will provide steel helmets for those who say "the roof will cave in if I ever come to church."

Blankets will be furnished for those who think that the church is too cold, and fans will be provided for those who think that the church is too hot.

There will be a special section with lounge chairs for those who feel that our seats are too hard for them.

We will distribute "STAMP OUT STEWARDSHIP" buttons for those who feel the church is always asking them for money.

Doctors and nurses will be present for those who plan to be sick on Sunday.

We will have hearing aids for those who think I speak too softly, and cotton balls for those who think I speak too loud.

Scorecards will be available for those who wish to list the hypocrites who are present.

Some relatives will be invited for those who like to go visiting on Sunday.

There will be TV dinners for those who claim they can't go to church and still have time to cook Sunday dinner.

One section of the church will be devoted to trees and grass for those who claim they "can only find God in nature."

Finally, we will give out ashes and palms, and the sanctuary will be decorated with both Christmas poinsettias and Easter lilies for those who have never seen the church without them. **NO EXCUSE SUNDAY! WHAT A TIMELY IDEA!**

Today's Gospel is an invitation. **ALMIGHTY GOD** really does invite us to a banquet, the banquet of eternal life in His kingdom of heaven. If the pope or the president or a famous magician invited us, I'm sure we'd clear our calendars. **So why do we look for flimsy excuses when God does the inviting? It just doesn't make any sense!**

This week, just give a little thought to what attitudes, what things, what events, what persons, what temptations keep you from responding wholeheartedly to God's invitation. **NOTHING SHOULD EVER KEEP US FROM GOD.** And if something ever does, then we should do something about it as soon as possible. There really are no good excuses when it comes to Almighty God's invitation. And it's not only an invitation to come to church, it's an invitation to live as God wants us to live.

And we need to respond each day that we live. We can't put it off until tomorrow. We don't have unlimited time. We live in a fragile world. We all need to be ready, and it is our daily response to doing God's will that get us ready. And worshiping God is part of that response, an important part.

ALMIGHTY GOD invites you to an eternity of happiness with Him in heaven. So, what's your excuse for not responding?

God bless you!

29th Sunday in Ordinary Time - "A"

19 October 2008

FIRST READING: Isaiah 45:1, 4-6
PSALM: Psalm 96: 1,3-5, 7-10
SECOND READING: 1 Thessalonians 1:1-5b
GOSPEL: Matthew 22:15-21

In the Gospel today, Jesus asks us to think about what allegiance we owe to God as compared with what we owe to anyone else.

This week was awesome, even by Laughlin standards! Besides the oatmeal raison cookies, custard pie, fresh ravioli, and Cinnabons, there were three MAJOR eating opportunities this week - the parish picnic last Sunday afternoon, an overpriced gourmet restaurant in Vegas on Wednesday, and the Laughlin Chefs' Food Fest here on Thursday.

The array of homemade foods at the picnic amazed me, much better than the sandwiches and salads back in New Jersey! I fell asleep smiling on Sunday night for sure! And the overpriced Vegas restaurant was a weird experience - fortunately a friend treated me to it - because the prices would have scared me away! While I ordered and enjoyed more normal foods, the menu items included such things as GRILLED OCTOPUS TENTACLES, WARM LAMB'S TONGUE, LAMB'S BRAIN, FENNEL DUSTED SWEETBREADS, AND PIGS' TAILS. The bottle of wine we shared was in the lower-priced range at $150 for the bottle! And, honestly, it didn't taste any better than the wine I buy for less than $5.00 a bottle! I guess I just don't have a developed wine palate!

But the most awesome eating experience of the week was the LAUGHLIN CHEFS' FOOD FEST on Thursday night! If you missed it, plan on being there next year for it! The money raised supports local charities, and the chefs from the Laughlin casinos prepare their specialties for all to share. I couldn't possibly list everything I enjoyed that night, but the SEAFOOD FONDEAUX, LOBSTER CAKE ON A FOCACCIA BUN, BANANA SPLIT CHEESECAKE, LOBSTER CREME BRULEE, LOBSTER TAMALE, and some AWESOME TRUFFLES FLAVORED WITH CHILI PEPPERS, PISTACHIOS, AND GRAND MARNIER will not be forgotten! And last night I got to enjoy Debbie Reynolds right here in this showroom! I never thought I'd be working in the same showroom as Debbie Reynolds. Laughlin just keeps getting better and better!

A long time ago back in New Jersey when I was a young priest, I was helping out on Sundays in a little suburban parish. Mrs. Fagin, at 95, was the oldest parishioner. And every Sunday she would climb the church steps with her three-pronged cane, and take her seat in the front of the church just as she had done for her whole life. I overheard from some of the other parishioners that Mrs. Fagin had been telling people that she really liked my sermons. And the more I thought about it, the more I knew I had to find out WHY she liked my sermons! Here I was a young priest with so little experience and this parish matriarch liked my sermons! I wondered how I had touched her. Was she impressed with my theological clarity? So one Sunday, I got up the courage to ask her. As she reached the top of the church steps and came into the church, I said, "Mrs. Fagin, I've heard that you like my sermons. Please, tell me what it is that you like about them?" And she looked me straight in the eye, planted her three-pronged cane squarely in front of me, and said, **"Because, Sonny, you're the only one around here I can hear!"**

I've thought about that incident a lot, and it occurs to me that sometimes you and I are the only ones that someone can hear when they are looking for a reason to believe and to have Faith. We're not all priests and we're not all preachers, but sometimes God uses people like us, and even people we don't expect, to be God's instruments in the world.

Today's readings are a good reminder to us of how God acts towards us and what God expects from us. We sometimes have developed our own preconceived idea of exactly how God should handle a certain situation in our lives or in the life of the world. GOD SHOULD CURE THAT DISEASE BY A MIRACLE, GOD SHOULD ERASE ALL POVERTY FROM THE EARTH, GOD SHOULD STOP ALL WARS AND VIOLENCE, GOD SHOULD MAKE SURE I KEEP MY JOB, GOD SHOULD MAKE SURE THE RIGHT CANDIDATES WIN IN THE COMING ELECTIONS, GOD SHOULD

MAKE HIS GOSPEL KNOWN IN THE WORLD. But what if God wants to accomplish these things and others in ways that we don't anticipate? Are we willing to work with God when His plans are different than our plans? As one wise person once quipped: **"Lots of people want to serve God, but only as His advisors!"**

Today's readings remind us that God acts in His own way - through the people He chooses, even unlikely people! God calls Cyrus, a pagan king, to restore Israel to its own homeland. God enables Paul and his companions to preach the Gospel with such power that people come to believe almost immediately. And in the Gospel today, Jesus does what He does so often when He is confronted with a question; He turns it around: "Is it lawful to pay the census tax to Caesar or not?" is the question. Jesus' answer: "Whose image is this and whose inscription? Then repay to Caesar what belongs to Caesar, and to God what belongs to God." His answer reminds us that we have to decide just what our allegiance to the government and to God demands of us. And the answer is not just a once-a-year thing - that we don't cheat on our rightful income taxes, that we pay our fair share - No, the answer is much more daily. Each one of us must be prepared to work with the instruments that God is using to heal the problems of the world, and even to BE such instruments if that is what God wants.

God can cure disease, God can erase poverty, God can stop wars and violence, God can make sure that the right candidates win the elections, and God can do all sorts of things in this world - **BUT APPARENTLY HE'S NOT GOING TO DO IT WITHOUT OUR COOPERATION.** Sometimes you and I are going to be the **ONLY PERSONS** that someone can hear with the message of God's truth and the message of Faith.

I surely don't know why God has such faith in us to do what is right, but God does have that faith in us. For our part, I guess, we shouldn't let Him down.

God bless you!

Father Charlie and Paul at the entrance to the Riverside

30th Sunday in Ordinary Time - "A"

26 October 2008

FIRST READING: Exodus 22:20-26
PSALM: Psalm 18:2-4, 47, 51
SECOND READING: 1 Thessalonians 1:5c-10
GOSPEL: Matthew 22:34-40

In the Gospel today, Jesus sums up the Law of God very nicely. We must love God with all we have, and we must love our neighbors as we love ourselves.

LAUGHLIN REPORT: another awesome week! Some of our parishioners have been traveling and brought back some incredible goodies for me including real maple syrup and sharp cheddar cheese and gouda cheese. And there were also chocolate chip muffins and cookies and grapes. And somehow I managed to get treated to meals at SEVEN different restaurants this week! (By the way, I think this is a record, even for me!) And one of them was a perfect lobster dinner with a portobello mushroom appetizer. And my best deal of the week, a friend of mine from NY moved to Vegas. He's a licensed massage therapist. So we worked a deal - I got a free massage and he got a free dinner! He stretched my arms like they have never been stretched before! Gosh, I have to work that deal again sometime! And I took my buddy Billy out for breakfast one morning. Billy and his wife have two very young children so Billy enjoyed being out just with me. After five minutes in the restaurant, he told me that this was the first time in years that he had sat so long at a table without someone spitting up food on him, or pulling off his glasses, or crying. So I reached over and pulled off his glasses! He wants me to take his wife out for breakfast next week so she can see what it is like to eat a meal without being disturbed. I love being out here in Laughlin! Why we even have a state holiday this Friday - NEVADA DAY! It celebrates the fact that 144 years ago, on October 31, 1864, Nevada became a state in the United States of America. Check out page 7 of our bulletin today. I've listed a few interesting items about our state. Even an extra holiday! **Laughlin just keeps getting better and better!**

With elections coming up in a few weeks, and with many new laws to be voted upon, it is interesting to notice some really strange laws that can be found (at least according to the Internet) in our United States. Here are a few examples of what I found in various states and cities:

In Alabama, it is illegal to wear a fake mustache in church if it causes laughter.

In Alaska, it is illegal to give any alcoholic beverage to a moose.

In Minnesota, it is illegal to tease a skunk. (And mighty stupid too!)

In Oklahoma, it is illegal to hunt for whales.

In Kansas, it is illegal to sell cherry pie a la mode on a Sunday.

In St. Louis, Missouri, it is illegal for a firefighter to rescue a woman wearing a nightgown. In order to be rescued, she must be fully clothed.

In Waterloo, Nebraska, barbers are forbidden to eat onions between 7:00 AM and 7:00 PM.

In Virginia City, Nevada, it is illegal to drive a camel on the highway.

In Hood River, Oregon, it is illegal to juggle without a license.

In Providence, Rhode Island, it is illegal to sell toothpaste and a toothbrush to the same customer on a Sunday.

In Memphis, Tennessee, it is illegal to give a piece of your pie to a fellow diner in a restaurant or to take any unfinished pie home. All pie must be eaten on the premises of the restaurant.

In Las Vegas, Nevada, it is illegal to pawn your own dentures.

In Baxley, Ohio, it is illegal to install and use a slot machine in an outhouse.

In Florida, there is a law that if an elephant is tied to a parking meter, it must pay the same fee as a car.

And, finally, in Nicholas County, West Virginia, it is illegal for a clergyman to tell jokes or humorous stories during church services (which is probably why I've never been assigned to any parishes in Nicholas County, West Virginia!)

One law that has never become outdated or silly is the **LAW OF GOD**. And Jesus sums up the **LAW OF GOD** in today's Gospel very simply: **"You shall love the Lord, your God, with all your heart, with all your soul, with all your mind, ...and you shall love your neighbor as yourself."**

I'm sure that we have all found it difficult to focus our hearts and souls and minds on any one thing at all. We're pulled in so many different directions all at once - our families, our jobs, our friends, our hobbies, our church, our government, etc. But the lesson that Jesus is teaching today is that if we can give our attention wholeheartedly to God, then we actually do become capable of giving our best selves not only to God, but to our neighbor as well.

We pray today that we might all learn to love God as we should so that we will be able to love our neighbors as we should. This is the LAW OF GOD for us. It is eternal and unchangeable. And we need to live by it. And we learn the law of God for us through our Catholic Church. That's just one of the many reasons why it is so important for us to be here each Sunday. We need to keep our attention on God. Otherwise, we end up wandering aimlessly in all different directions.

If we put ourselves into the Presence of God, it will make a difference in our own lives and in the lives of our families, our parish and our whole community. It will help us to love the Lord, our God, with all our hearts and souls and minds. And if we can do that, then surely we will be learning to love our neighbor as ourselves. But it all starts with God. We can't do it on our own.

Take the time to pray every day. And make the effort to come and pray in the Presence of God every Sunday. It's worth more that we can ever imagine. And it can change the world!

God bless you!

All Souls Day - "A"

2 November 2008

FIRST READING: Wisdom 3:1-9
PSALM: Psalm 23:1-6
SECOND READING: Romans 5:5-11
GOSPEL: John 6:37-40

In the Gospel today, Jesus promises eternal life to those who follow Him.

The Laughlin Report continues to be awesome! Why I even heard that New Jersey had 14 inches of snow this past Tuesday! And it was still in October! I sure am glad I'm out here where I don't have to shovel sunshine! And the food this week has been exceptional! Pasta with a great tomato sauce, seafood salad stuffed into ripe tomatoes, homemade bread, home-grown sliced pears in homemade syrup, fried chicken breasts and a platter of assorted pastries, chocolate chip cookies, pumpkin pie, and an amazing chocolate cake made with sauerkraut and beer! I never knew beer could taste so good! And I also received a pair of Pittsburgh Steelers socks (which I'm wearing). I was told that it might be good luck for the team if I wear them. Didn't know my feet were so important! And the visitors keep coming, for which all of us are so glad. Last month, we were averaging about 200 people at Mass each weekend ahead of last year at the same time. The parish and the local economy thank each and every one of you for visiting Laughlin! Come back again, and again! And bring your friends!

My Mom loved Laughlin as much as I do. And we started coming here back in 1990. It's grown a lot since then, but it still is a magical place in my mind and heart.

When my Mom died back in 2006, I received nearly 700 emails/letters/cards and messages from my friends, and thousands of words of comfort were spoken to me by people in my parish and the surrounding area. Someday I'm going to put some of them together into a little booklet because I think they might be helpful for other people who have to face the death of someone they love. One of the most memorable scenes was an encounter with a young student at our parish school. A few weeks after my Mom died, Adam (in the 5th grade) saw me at the school and came up to me, grabbed my hand, and said, **"Father Charlie, I'm so sorry that your Mom died."** And I was really impressed with his sincerity. Then, still holding my hand tightly, he continued, **"But she's in a better place."** And again, I was impressed that our little school had taught this young man such an important truth. But he was still holding my hand, so I knew he had more to say. He looked me in the eye and continued to speak saying, **"And you'll be with her soon."** Well, my first thought was, **"MAYBE NOT TOO SOON, BUT EVENTUALLY!"** And then I realized that this young man had learned one of the most important truths of our Catholic Faith - that life never ends! That for those who are faithful, we never lose the ones we love, and someday (maybe not TOO soon!), we will be together with them again.

Today is All Souls Day, a day on which Catholics and many other Christians prayerfully remember their friends and relatives who have died. At all of our Masses this weekend, we will be praying for **All the Faithful Departed.** We really believe that we assist them in their transition from this life to eternal life with God. And as Catholics, we do firmly believe in eternal life. We know that death is not the end. But still, it is not an easy topic to consider. Some families never take their children to wakes because they don't want to expose them to death. That's really kind of sad. Death is a part of life, and it really would be better for children to be at a wake for one of their parents' friends or neighbors than to have their Mom or Dad or Grandma or Grandpa be the first person they ever see laid out at a wake.

We all shy away from talking about death. As one old Italian priest in Brooklyn said at a funeral some years ago, **"Everybody wants to go to heaven, but nobody wants to go now."**

For All Souls Day this year, I wanted to talk about death in a way that we could not only understand, but also appreciate. We've listened to our Scripture readings, but I wanted something a bit more understandable for our emotions and our hearts. I found something on the Internet that really appealed to me, and I share it with you as we pray for **All the Faithful Departed** this weekend:

Found in the dead soldier's shirt pocket, over his heart, was a newspaper clipping which the young man had apparently always carried with him. His buddy opened it, read it, and cried again. The clipping said so much about what his friend believed about death and life.

So he sent the clipping home to the dead soldier's parents, that they might be comforted by what their son believed, that his faith might help to strengthen their faith. The clipping read something like this:

We are standing on a shore. A large sailing ship is about to pull out. Friends and relatives of ours are standing on the deck, waving goodbye, throwing streamers, calling to us, calling our names. And we call to them, and to each other, **"Look, there's Grandma...there's Aunt Helen...there's Uncle Bill."** A bell sounds and the ship begins to move away from the shore.

We stand silently for a very long time and we watch as the ship goes further and further away until, finally, the mast is just a vertical pencil line on the distant horizon. Then it too goes down, until we can no longer see it. And we sigh, **"Oh, she's gone."**

But gone from where? Gone from our sight. That's all.

For at the very moment we sigh, **"Oh, she's gone,"** someone on another shore is jumping up and down, laughing and yelling and pointing excitedly out to sea saying, **"Look! She's coming! Look, the ship is coming home! There's Grandma...there's Aunt Helen...there's Uncle Bill."**

The ship is coming home. There is another shore, another dimension in which we have already begun to live. Because of our Catholic Faith, we are filled with the Spirit of our Risen Savior forever.

On this All Souls Day, we might be a little sad as we remember those who have died. But we also should be a little happy that they are finally home with God. And someday, God willing, we will all be together again.

God bless you!

Father Charlie and Bishop Joseph A. Pepe after administering the Sacrament of Confirmation.

Dedication of the Lateran Basilica

9 November 2008

FIRST READING: Ezekiel 47:1-2, 8-9, 12
PSALM: Psalm 46:2-3, 5-6, 8-9
SECOND READING: 1 Corinthians 3:9c-11, 16-17
GOSPEL: John 2:13-22

In the Gospel today, Jesus declares that the temple is His Father's house and must be respected.

Well, it's been another great week in Laughlin! I've been enjoying the extra hour of sleep, but still getting confused when I have to go over to Arizona now that the time is different over there. Had some wonderful baked potatoes stuffed with scrambled eggs and bacon, some honey buns, eggplant parmegiana, melt-in-your-mouth gnocchi, and a stuffed artichoke. Picked up a cold during the week, but thanks to a batch of homemade miracle-working chicken soup, I'm pretty much over that now! And apparently, the Pittsburgh Steelers won their game last week only because I was wearing the team socks, so now I'm supposed to wear Steelers' socks every weekend throughout the season. Okay, I'll do it today, but it wouldn't be fair to the other teams if I did it EVERY weekend! If my feet are that lucky, maybe I could auction them off to the highest bidder? Maybe my slogan could be: **"Rent my soles while I work to save your souls!"** Kind of catchy, isn't it?

Over the years, our United States military forces have used a number of sayings/slogans to capture their essence. Everyone can remember the Army's TV ad: **"BE ALL YOU CAN BE."** Or the Navy's: **"IT'S NOT JUST A JOB, IT'S AN ADVENTURE."** Or the one from the Air Force: **"AIM HIGH...NOTHING CAN STOP THE U.S. AIR FORCE."** And most people should know that the Coast Guard's motto is **"SEMPER PARATUS"** - **"ALWAYS PREPARED."** But certainly no saying is more famous than the U.S. Marine Corps': **"SEMPER FI"-"SEMPER FIDELIS"-"ALWAYS FAITHFUL."**

It is undeniable how much we as U.S. citizens owe to the courage and the loyalty and the idealism of the men and women who have served throughout our nation's history in the armed forces. As Veterans Day is celebrated this week on Tuesday, November 11th, it is good for us to remember all our veterans, and to thank those veterans who are here with us at Mass today. So if you have served in our nation's military forces, I ask you to please stand up for us to bless and thank you today.....(applause)

And, veterans, you are a living lesson for all of us. One of the goals of the military training which every Soldier, Sailor, Airman, Coast Guardsman or Marine receives is a training in wisdom, in being ready for whatever circumstances might come up. Our forces are taught not only to react, but more importantly, to plan, to think, to be aware of consequences. They are taught to be prepared. This is a good thing for them, and for our whole nation. Every veteran knows that there is no substitute for being prepared. Every Catholic should know the same thing. There is no substitute for the firm foundation that only our Catholic Faith can give us. That's why we come to church, that's why we pray, that's why we are here today at Mass.

Today's Feast of the Dedication of the Lateran Basilica in Rome dates back to the 4th century when the Laterani Family donated the site to the Catholic Church and a church was built and dedicated. It predates St. Peter's Basilica and is the original church of the popes. It is considered the "Mother Church" of all Catholic Churches throughout the world. So as we celebrate today's feast here in Laughlin, we are celebrating the importance of sacred places in our varied towns and throughout the world, and throughout our lives.

Normally a church is a building that looks different from other buildings in our lives. It's not easily confused with homes or schools or stores or restaurants. Of course, here in Laughlin, church for us is sometimes a casino showroom at the Riverside. Casinos have lights and bells, and so do churches. And, as one dealer told me, do you know the difference between a man praying in a casino and a man praying in a church? **The man praying in the casino really means what he says!** (Just a little casino/church humor!). And people really do put casino chips and slot tickets into our collections, and I really do cash them in for the church each week by visiting the casinos, and people really have referred to me as the "chip" monk!

But seriously, folks, when we gather at the River-side for Mass, we are just as really in church as folks gathering at St. Peter's Basilica in Rome. As one person commented, **"When the priest comes down the aisle, we're not in a casino anymore, we're in a church."**

We are here today because we recognize that this is a sacred place. We know that God is present and we have come to share in His worship with those others in our community who recognize God dwelling here in this place.

Today's feast is a celebration for all our sacred places throughout our lives. I'd like to speak about a couple of things that this feast suggests to me:

1. Look around this church and think of all the churches you have attended in the course of your lives.....think of how many hundreds and thousands of people have been baptized, confirmed, given First Holy Communion, married and buried from these sacred places in our lives. We come into a sacred place for all the really important events in our lives. If church walls could talk, imagine the stories of faith that we would hear! Imagine all the people who gained courage by spending time in a church with the Lord and seeking His guidance. Imagine all the people over the years who have quietly prayed here and placed their health in God's hands. Imagine all the children who first received Jesus in Holy Communion around this

altar. Churches are places which are sacred to the memories of all of us. Listen carefully to our prayers, particularly our mention of those who are sick or in need. Even those who can't be with us are remembered here.

2. Look at the people gathered here today. We have the very young and the very old, and just about every age in between. I could pick a number between 1 and 91, and we would probably have someone here today who is that age. We have people here who have been coming into this building for years, and people who are here today for the very first time. We have people here who we know are living saints, and we have people here who can barely escape from their sins. And you know what's truly amazing? That God wants all of us to be here with Him. Most of us haven't been invited to dinner with the president or with the bishop, but all of us have been invited here for this supper with the God Who created the whole universe.

3. Look at the altar and the tabernacle. In a few moments, Christ will become present on our altar through the words of consecration. We will be invited to receive Him in Holy Communion. And He will remain in our tabernacle for every hour of every day. Certainly today's feast honors a particular church in Rome. But it also reminds us that we don't have to go to Rome to find a sacred place. We have one right here in Laughlin. And we always have one near us wherever we travel.

As you leave church today, give thanks to God that we live in a country which allows us to have these sacred places. And maybe just once in the next couple of weeks, plan to stop in a church in addition to Sunday Mass, and spend a few moments in the presence of the Lord. Putting yourself in the presence of the Lord is an important component of our Christian life. Think of the strength and the help that only God can give.

That's basically what Faith comes down to, isn't it? The realization that we need God, that there are some things that only God can give to us, and we need to place ourselves in the presence of God frequently. This is indeed a holy place. For God's sake as well as your own, make sure you know that your presence is expected in this sacred place not because God **needs** us, but because God **wants** us, and because we **need** God. That's basically what Faith comes down to, isn't it? The realization that we need God. We do. We really do.

God bless you!

33rd Sunday in Ordinary Time - "A"

16 November 2008

FIRST READING: Proverbs 31:10-13, 19-20, 30-31
PSALM: Psalm 128:1-5
SECOND READING: 1 Thessalonians 5:1-6
GOSPEL: Matthew 25:14-30

In the Gospel today, Jesus teaches yet another parable about a man who leaves various sums of money to be used in his absence and how each one is accountable for his actions.

I've been here for almost 5 months now, and it just keeps getting better and better! Love the little breeze we're having. Was a little disappointed to hear that the Steelers lost last weekend despite my wearing their socks, but maybe my feet are destined to help another team. I missed the Hobo Stew on Wednesday night, but I got to the Chamber of Commerce mixer on Thursday night and ate my way through some awesome shrimp with a sweet walnut sauce. Enjoyed some beans and ham, tuna salad, homemade fudge, and scorching fried hot peppers. But the most unusual food I got this week was DEEP-FRIED DILL PICKLES! A friend brought them over and we sat up until 2:00 AM eating them! Never knew a dill pickle could be deep-fried! And I was lucky on a penny slot machine..... got 14 wilds on a free spin and walked away with nearly $650.00. Now that's the story I will be telling for a long time to come!

Most of our parishioners know that I taught junior high and high school for 16 years as a priest. It was a challenging and thoroughly enjoyable assignment. One of the things I learned from my students is that sometimes the best way to teach them is by telling them a story. They kind of naturally listened to the story, they thought about it, and many times they actually remembered the lesson it was intended to teach.

Interestingly enough, basic teaching methodology supports what I learned in the classroom. There are three key words why stories work so well in the classroom: ATTENTION, REFLECTION, and RETENTION. Stories hold our attention, invite us to think, and help us to remember the lessons we have learned.

Sometimes the stories were "made-up", like the time I told my 7th graders about the little boy in the 7th grade who was sent to the principal's office because he kept talking in class.....and he was never heard from again! His parents are still looking for him!

And I remember my first pastor, Father McGarry. I put that man through so much! He wanted to do something with the teens so I took him roller skating with us when he was nearly 70 years old! He fell and hurt his back. He told me he thought I was deliberately trying to kill him! I kept apologizing to him and asked if there was ANYTHING I could do that might help. He said that a mustard plaster would make him feel better. So I set out to find a mustard plaster, eventually locating a box of it at an old downtown drugstore. I came home so very happy with that package, and told Father McGarry to lay down on his bed. I mixed up the ingredients and slathered the plaster on his back, and then left him to rest with the warm mixture on his back. Unfortunately, I had never bothered to read the rest of the directions which said something about **"CAUTION: NEVER LEAVE A MUSTARD PLASTER ON A PERSON'S SKIN FOR MORE THAN 10 MINUTES!"** So when I came back to Father's room about two hours later, he was writhing in burning pain, and I had to chip the plaster off his blistered back using a screwdriver! Then he was SURE I was trying to kill him!

Funny, but I actually do remember Father McGarry telling me stories about the recalcitrant young priest who was sent to some obscure parish out in Wisconsin and never heard from again! Sometimes the stories were true, actual life experiences. Sometimes, I hoped they were made-up! All in all, they were a very interesting way to teach.

When I started preaching in a parish, I found that the same methodology continued to work. In fact, I think it works well even with adults today. After all, you are still listening to me, right?

Jesus was a Master Teacher. He knew that telling His "students" a story would hold their attention, would invite their reflection, and hopefully would help them to remember the lessons He had taught. **That is why Jesus so frequently taught by using parables, stories that hold our attention, cause us to think, and hopefully help us to remember the lessons that Jesus wants to teach us.** Remember these words: **ATTENTION, REFLECTION** and **RETENTION.**

Today's Gospel is a parable. It's an interesting story about a man and his servants to whom he had entrusted various amounts of money. Then he left them for awhile to see what they would do. When he returned, he asked for an accounting of what they had done with his money, the talents he had given to them. Two out of the three had multiplied the amount, one had buried it and just gave it back untouched and unused. The master praises the industrious servants, and gives them even greater responsibilities. But he condemns the one who hid his money as "WICKED" and "LAZY" (in an older translation, that servant is called a "WORTH-LESS LAZY LOUT.")

The story holds our attention even if we have heard it many times before. It invites our reflection about what we do with the talents that God has given to us. And it hopefully helps us to remember the lessons that Jesus was teaching us - that we need to use our God-given talents. It doesn't matter one bit if we have received a lot or a little. All of it is a gift from God. What are we doing with the gifts that God has given to us?

The next time you hear a Gospel parable, think about those three words: ATTENTION, REFLECTION and RETENTION. See if they don't help you to get something worthwhile from the parable. After all, Jesus is still the Master Teacher, and all of us are still His students. And hopefully we're really good learners.

God bless you!

Just one of the many types of transportation available in Laughlin!

Christ the King

23 November 2008

FIRST READING: Ezekiel 34:11-12, 15-17
PSALM: Psalm 23:1-3, 5-6
SECOND READING: 1 Corinthians 15:20-26, 28
GOSPEL: Matthew 25:31-46

In the Gospel today, Jesus reminds us that we will all be judged by God on the basis of how we have treated one another.

Another week in Paradise! (Also known as Laughlin!) Pat, who was my secretary in New Jersey is visiting Nevada this week, so I drove up to Las Vegas on Wednesday to meet her. I parked my car at the hotel where she was staying and was heading into the casino to meet her when I ended up in an elevator with two couples on vacation. They thought I worked there because I looked so "official" as they said! So I told them that I'm a local, from Laughlin. And, of course, I encouraged them to come and visit Laughlin during their vacation. They sort of sneered, and said, **"Laughlin? There's no good food in Laughlin!"** Trust me, by the time we reached the ground floor, they had heard a lot about the good food in Laughlin! Man, they were just in the wrong place at the wrong time if they wanted to put down the food here in Laughlin! The Visitor's Bureau would have been proud of me! Why just this week, I had a perfect lobster tail, a pumpkin roll with cream cheese filling, homemade banana bread with chocolate chips, fruit-filled jello, apple crisp, orange roughy, fried peppers, turkey soup, and so much more! I can only imagine what it will be like when the Christmas baking starts! Oh, and I found a place that does a complete oil change including a new filter for only $15.00. I love a bargain! It just keeps getting better and better here! And I intend to keep telling you about it each and every week!

By now, my parishioners know a lot about me, but here's one thing you may not know yet.....I love country music! I love the story-telling within most country songs, and I love the titles of some of the songs too. How can anyone not love some of these country classics?:

"You Struck Out in the Ballpark of My Mind"
"Dropkick Me, Jesus, Through the Goalposts of Life"
"I've Flushed You from the Outhouse of My Heart"
"I've Got Red Eyes from Your White Lies and I'm Blue All the Time"
"Her Teeth Were Stained, But Her Heart Was Pure"
"If My Nose Were Full of Nickels, I'd Blow It All on You"
"If Whiskey Were a Woman, I'd Be Married for Sure"
"If You Don't Leave Me Alone, I'll Go and Find Someone Who Will"
"If You Can't Bite, Don't Growl"
"How Can I Miss You If You Won't Go Away?"

"I'm So Miserable Without You, It's Like Having You Here"
"I've Been Roped and Throwed By Jesus in the Holy Spirit Corral"
"Here's a Quarter, Call Someone Who Cares"
"I'm Just a Bug on the Windshield of Life"
"I Still Miss You, Baby, But My Aim's Getting Better"

One of my favorite old country sons is from the early 1980's by Randy Travis. It's called **"What Are You Going to Do About Me?"**

The song tells a really interesting story. This guy is in love with this girl, but she leaves him. And he wants her back more than anything else in the world. In the song, he promises that he'll follow her everywhere, he'll try anything he knows just to win her back. He even describes the scene if she tries to date some other guy.....he'll be hiding out on her back porch with a baseball bat to clobber the other guy after the date! He tells her he will always be there, and the refrain in the song repeatedly asks her the question: "What are you going to do about me?"

As we celebrate the **FEAST OF CHRIST THE KING** once again, it seems to me that those words would fit very well on Jesus' own lips as He speaks to us at Mass today. "What are you going to do about Me?" Sometimes I think we try to get away from Jesus, to get out of doing what we know He really wants us to do. And yet, if we really believe what we celebrate today, if we really believe that Jesus is the King of the whole universe, the Savior of the world, the One Who loves us so much that He even died on the cross for us, then we have to come to terms with His place in our lives.

WHAT ARE YOU GOING TO DO ABOUT ME when you see Me in need of food or clothing?

WHAT ARE YOU GOING TO DO ABOUT ME when you meet Me as a stranger at work, in school, in town?

WHAT ARE YOU GOING TO DO ABOUT ME when you see Me dying of cancer, sick with loneliness, disoriented by Alzheimer's?

WHAT ARE YOU GOING TO DO ABOUT ME when you know I need you to uphold My teachings, to be faithful to your families, to practice the Faith I have freely given to you in Baptism?

WHAT ARE YOU GOING TO DO ABOUT ME when I need you?

What a difference in our lives it would make if we really began to believe that Jesus is our King, that He really does have the first claim on our minds and our hearts and our time and our resources. All that we have ultimately comes from Him. He is our King and so much more.

I think that if we listen carefully, we can all hear Jesus asking us individually today that powerful question, **"WHAT ARE YOU GOING TO DO ABOUT ME?"**

It's a great question, an important question, and Jesus is waiting for our answer.

God bless you!

First Sunday of Advent - "B"

30 November 2008

FIRST READING: Isaiah 63:16b-17m 19b; 64:2-7
PSALM: Psalm 80:2-3, 15-16, 18-19
SECOND READING: 1 Corinthians 1:3-9
GOSPEL: Mark 13:33-37

In the Gospel today, Jesus warns His followers to be alert and watchful.

I like to think of myself as a professional eater. If eating were an Olympic event, I'd be coming home with the gold every time! Well, for a professional eater like me, Thanksgiving Week in awesome! And Thanksgiving Week in Laughlin is even more awesome! It's like being surrounded by people who just want to feed me! Even prior to Thanksgiving Day, there were delicious asparagus and cheese crepes, apple sauce cake, fried chicken and biscuits. Up in Vegas on Tuesday, I baptized the daughter of some friends of mine from Louisiana, so back at their house after the Baptism, we had homemade red beans and rice to celebrate. And then, just before Thanksgiving, there was a huge pumpkin pie cake and boxes of Cinnabons. And then, the turkey day feast itself with all the trimmings! I still can taste the stuffing and the walnut pie and the mint chocolate chip cookies. And the baby carrots with cashew nuts and raisons. I have so much for which to be thankful here in Laughlin! And I hope every one here with us today can say the same. It's good to deliberately remember how blessed we all are, and how thankful we should be. And I'm not only talking about the food. I'm talking about all the blessings of family and friends in our lives.

Each year, it starts a little earlier, each year it catches us off-guard. But it happens over and over again throughout our country. I'm speaking of the displaying of the signs of the Christmas Season. It used to be that stores and malls waited at least until Thanksgiving Weekend to really rev up the annual shopping frenzy, but in recent years, the idea of Christmas shopping has relentlessly crept earlier and earlier to the week before Thanksgiving, to the beginning of November, to the day after Halloween, and even, GASP!, to the middle of October which is when I started noticing Santa and snowmen and Christmas music in some of the stores.

And then there is that generically bland, but oh so politically correct greeting, **"Happy Holidays"** that has all but drowned out the much older and much more historically correct **"Merry Christmas"** in American society. It's getting so ridiculous that one of my friends even coined a word for people to use who want to be even more politically correct. He suggests that we combine Christmas, Hanukkah, and Kwanza into one universal greeting, and that we then wish each other a **"Merry Chrismahanuk-kawanza!"**

As Catholic Christians, we are not preparing to celebrate the "winter solstice" or the "winter holidays" or any other generically-named festival. We are preparing to celebrate the annual remembrance of one particular historical event on December 25th - the birth of Jesus Christ, the Savior of the World, in Bethlehem, some 2000 years ago.

Loudly and clearly, we need to proclaim our faith in Jesus Christ, and all that Christmas celebrates about God Himself becoming a part of the human race and living on this planet for some 33 years before giving His life on the cross for the salvation of the world. As important as Easter is, Christmas is vitally important in the history of salvation too. In fact, it is absolutely true to say, that if there were no Christmas, there would be no Easter either!

We must not let Christmas be taken away from us. As nice as trees and snowmen and lights and reindeer and Santa might be, the true symbol of Christmas is the Nativity Scene - the manger with Jesus, Mary and Joseph, the sheep and the cattle, the shepherds, the wise men and the camels, and, of course, the Christmas star.

And certainly the world situation prompts us to focus our thoughts on the peace that only Jesus Christ can bring. We need to pray fervently and frequently that the message of peace and hope that Jesus brought into the world on that first Christmas Day will somehow overcome the violence and unrest in our world community. This week's horrific Islamic terrorist attack in Mumbai, India, reminds us how much the world needs the peace of Jesus Christ.

Jesus is the Reason for the season. Christmas without Jesus is just unthinkable. We're so fortunate. We not only know WHAT Christmas celebrates, but we know WHO Christmas celebrates. As we go through these weeks of preparation, let's keep alert and awake and know that without Jesus, there would be no Christmas for anyone. Advent begins today - let's start getting our homes and hearts and minds and souls ready for Christmas. It will be here sooner than we can imagine. Let's make it the best Christmas ever!

God bless you!

Second Sunday of Advent - "B"

7 December 2008

FIRST READING: Isaiah 40:1-5, 9-11
PSALM: Psalm 85:9-14
SECOND READING: 2 Peter 3:8-14
GOSPEL: Mark:1-8

In the Gospel today, St. John the Baptist acknowledges his mission as the "voice of one crying out in the desert" to prepare the way of the Lord.

What a week in Laughlin! Last Sunday afternoon, I went to a piano recital at the Laughlin Library. Great cookies.....and great Christmas music too! On Friday night, we had over 290 people at our parish Christmas party. Great food, great music, great dancing, and a really fun group of people! Dancing to the "YMCA" was fun.....and brought back some really cool memories to me of when a friend of mine dragged me on stage, put a feather headdress on me, and had me join in a Village People impersonation in front of 1600 people. But that's a story for another Sunday.....

One couple even handed me a package of homemade peanut brittle as they entered the party, and then I had strawberry bread, homemade potato pie, lemon pie, a Wisconsin cheesecake, along with turkey soup, homemade crisp dill pickles and pickled peppers. I even got invited to dinner one night by a vacationing couple who had been at Mass last weekend, and thought they should take a turn at feeding me! And yesterday, I found a brand new restaurant in Bullhead City with great food and huge portions right on Route 95.

But the best thing this week was when I went into a store and the clerk proofed me for my age before she would give me my "Senior Citizen" discount! I've never been proofed! I've always looked older than I really am! I guess she was just trying to be nice.....but it sure felt good to have to prove that I'm a senior citizen! Never in a million years did I think I'd ever get to do that! This is a great time in my life!

"Do not ignore this one fact, beloved, that with the Lord one day is like a thousand years, and a thousand years is like one day. The Lord does not delay His promise." So writes St. Peter in today's Second Reading.

There's a wonderful story of a man praying to God, and it goes like this:

"God," says the man.
"Yes," says God.
"Can I ask You a question?"
"Go right ahead."
"God, what is a million years to You?"
"A million years to Me is only a second."
"HHmmm...God, what is a million dollars to You?"
"A million dollars to Me is like a penny."
"God, can I have a penny?"
"Sure.....just a second."

Life doesn't always happen at the speed with which we want it to happen. Things sometimes take more time and more effort than we anticipated. And sometimes it is easy to get discouraged when things don't happen the way we want them to happen, or as fast as we want them to happen. It's good for us to remember the wisdom of St. Peter in today's Second Reading......that God's timing is different than our own. But that things will happen in God's time, without delay.

The people in Israel waited for centuries for the coming of the Savior, and in God's own good time, Jesus came, was born, and lived among them. St. John the Baptist in today's Gospel comes to prepare the way for the Lord. He called people to get ready for the coming of the Savior. He knew that Jesus was coming and he wanted the people to be ready.

You and I are in a similar situation as we approach Christmas. We know that Jesus is coming, and we know we need to get things ready. Oh, it might take more time and more effort than we had planned, but it is certainly worth every bit of time and effort we can put into it, because it will surely happen whether we're ready or not.

So besides writing cards, buying and wrapping gifts, putting up beautiful decorations, preparing cookies, we also need to get our hearts and minds and souls ready for Christmas. For those who have been faithful, we just need to keep on being faithful and watchful. For those who have been lazy, we need to get ourselves back to the practice of our Catholic Faith while there is still time. Showing up on Christmas unprepared is not very smart. The Savior of the world is coming, and we need to get ready. Christmas is only a couple of weeks away, and things in our lives should be different because of Jesus coming into our world.

God bless you!

Third Sunday of Advent - "B"

14 December 2008

FIRST READING: Isaiah 61:1-2a, 10-11
PSALM: Luke 1:46-50, 53-54
SECOND READING: 1 Thessalonians 5:16-24
GOSPEL: John 1:6-8, 19-28

In the Gospel today, St. John the Baptist declares that he is not the Christ, but that he is the one who will prepare the way for the Christ.

The Laughlin Report: 1.25 million homes in the Northeast were without power this week because of a huge ice storm that hit the area. **I love living in Laughlin where there is a zero percent chance of an ice storm!** My week started with a shrimp cocktail on Sunday night, and continued with awesome rice balls, tomato soup, garlic mashed potatoes, and my first Christmas fruitcake of the season! Then some whiskey-glazed chicken, brownies, carrot cake, pumpkin cream cheese roll, and some homemade cookies. A crazy friend of mine is making a YouTube video called **"Shoe on the Head"** rap, so he's asking all his friends to send him pictures of themselves balancing a shoe on their heads. So at 11:00 PM one night, I tried taking my picture while balancing a shoe on my head. That's actually a lot harder to do than it sounds! And while I was doing it, my friend Flash called and asked what I was doing. So I said, **"I'm trying to take a picture of myself**

while balancing a shoe on my head." There was a long awkward pause and then he said, **"Should I be calling someone to come over and check on you?"** It is so much fun living here! And have you seen the sunsets recently? They're incredible!

My alarm clock goes off at 5:17 AM each morning, but I don't usually head up to bed until about midnight or later, so it is usually not a problem for me to fall asleep as soon as I hit the bed. However, I do keep a pile of magazines near my bed in case I need a little something to read before drifting off to sleep. Recently, I picked up an article called **"The Shy Guy's Guide to Dating"** and it had a section on the **"10 best pick-up lines"**, but I really don't have much use for them. And I'm not sure that they would work if I did have a use for them! I thought I'd share a few with you today:

1. I forgot my phone number.....can I have yours?
2. I hope you know CPR, because you just took my breath away.
3. If I followed you home, would you keep me?
4. If water were beauty, you would be the ocean!
5. Do you believe in love at first sight? Or should I walk by again?
6. I must be a snowflake because I've fallen for you.
7. Hi, the voices in my head told me to come over and talk to you.

They even included a section on comebacks for unwanted pick-up lines:

"So, baby, your place or mine?"
"Both...you go to your place and I'll go to mine!"

"Haven't I seen you someplace before?"
"Yes, that's why I don't go there anymore!"

"Is this seat empty?"
"Yes, and this one will be too if you sit down!"

I did find one article on the topic of how we identify ourselves. There were some funny sections like the ones on **"Which character in the Simpsons are you?"** or **"Which Harry Potter character are you?"** But there was also an interesting one about going up to a person and just asking him the question: **"Who are you?"** and seeing how he responds. Supposedly, the response is a key to his personality. For example, if the person responds to **"Who are you?"** with **"I'm Joe,"** it indicates a friendly, open personality. If the response is **"Mr. Joseph Smith,"** then a more formal, reticent personality is indicated. If the response is **"None of your business!",** then you can presume that the person doesn't really want a friendly relationship with you! The responses could also be things like **"I'm an American"** showing pride in our country, or **"I'm a mechanic"** showing pride in his work, or **"I'm a mother"** showing identification with her family. It made for some interesting reading.

Several times in today's Gospel, John the Baptist is asked the same question, **"Who are you?"** And this was certainly not a pop psychology quiz. The priests and the Levites sent from Jerusalem were deadly serious. If John the Baptist really was the Messiah, the long-awaited One, this was a matter of life and death for the nation. They waited on his response and they questioned him over and over.

"I am not the Messiah. I am not the Christ. I am not Elijah. I am not the Prophet. I am the voice of one crying in the desert, make straight the way of the Lord." John the Baptist knew exactly who he was and what God wanted him to do. John's whole life had been a preparation for the coming of the Lord.

The Lord is still trying to come into this world, still trying to have mankind accept His kingdom and His salvation. The Lord is still in need of people like John the Baptist, people who know exactly who they are and what God wants of them, people who are willing to prepare the way for the Lord to come into the hearts and minds and souls of mankind.

As Christmas 2008 approaches, take just a moment today from your Christmas buying and wrapping and card-writing and decorating, and just ask yourself this question: "Who am I?" and see if this answer might fit: **"I am a voice for the Lord in my family and among my friends. I am preparing myself and my world for the Lord's coming. By my prayers each day, by my worship at Mass each Sunday, by the way that I live and speak, I am bringing my family and my friends closer to Jesus."**

God bless you!

For many people in my generation, it was the religious Sisters who taught us in our Catholic grammar school days or in our CCD classes. I didn't have a lay teacher until I got into high school. And I can still remember the names of every one of the Sisters who taught me in grammar school: Sister Paul Joseph, Sister Ann Dorothy, Sister Marie Eugene, Sister Cecilia Veronica, Sister Teresa Aloysia, Sister John Bernard, Sister Flavian, Sister St. Gerald, and Sister Angelina. To some extent, I owe my practice of the Catholic Faith to them. And so do many of us. So it is not a difficult thing to ask for generosity in this annual Collection for the Retired Religious to take care of the needs of the retired religious men and women throughout these United States. Please be generous in our second collection today for them.

Fourth Sunday of Advent - "B"

21 December 2008

FIRST READING: 2 Samuel 7:1-5, 8b-12, 14a, 16
PSALM: Psalm 89:2-5, 27, 29
SECOND READING: Romans 16:25-27
GOSPEL: Luke 1:26-38

In the Gospel today, the Angel Gabriel comes to Mary and announces that she will be the Mother of God.

I'm still busy unpacking all my cartons of stuff from New Jersey. Several people have commented that I must have unpacked the cartons filled with snow this week! Even Father Kevin, the Vicar General of the Las Vegas Diocese, commented on Friday that I was probably the cause of this week's snowstorms in the area! I don't think I can take credit for that! I was up in Vegas for the snowstorm and the roads back to Laughlin were blocked at Searchlight and on Highway 163 by Christmas Tree Pass. It felt so weird to think that I couldn't get back to Laughlin! But fortunately snow melts out here. If we had snow like this in New Jersey, it would hang around on the ground for a few weeks before melting. During the snowstorm, a buddy of mine up in Vegas decided to make dinner for him and me, but realized that he only had one plate and one fork...so we had to head out to the local store to buy some plates and silverware. He made an awesome cream cheese and fresh garlic cream sauce over some pasta, and then we watched the snow fall and sat far apart so we wouldn't breathe our garlic-filled breath on each other. Also had some great mandarin orange salad, broccoli cheese casserole, tuna salad, corn muffins, lemon squares and baklava this week. If good food keeps coming in this week at such a fast pace, I'm afraid my sermon next week will sound like a menu!

I like to think that I do a pretty good job as a priest, but I have actually been told that I do my best in another job. You already know that I love magic, but doing magic isn't what I do best. In fact, I haven't been able to learn a single decent magic trick at all.....but I'm still trying. I even have my Lance Burton 100 Magic Trick set! I've known Lance since before he was famous in Las Vegas and on TV. He's even remarked publicly that I've seen his show more often than anyone who doesn't actually work for the show. But his best comment was: **"Charlie, you make the best audience member for a magic show. You don't come to figure out the tricks; you come to be amazed. That's precisely the audience a magician is looking for. And you never miss the magic. It's always amazing to you."**

I was thinking of that as I was writing Lance's Christmas card this week. And it occurred to me that the same concept might be true in other areas of our lives. For instance, why do we come to church every Sunday? Do we come to critique the sermon or to see if the music fits our tastes? Do we come because our family makes us come?

Do we come because we want people to think we are holy? Or rather, do we come because we know that God is here and that God is going to amaze us with His generosity to us? If the sermon bores us, or the music isn't what we think it should be, of if the person sitting next to us smells like wet dog fur, so what? God is still here and God is still offering us more than we could possibly deserve. On the other hand, if the music is uplifting and the sermon thrills our souls, and the person sitting next to us smells like a forest in springtime, well, that is just some extra icing on the cake. It makes something already wonderful even more wonderful. The attitude with which we come to Mass on Sunday certainly affects us. Why, with the wrong attitude, we could even miss the magic!

And what about Christmas coming in only four more days.....could we miss the magic of Christmas because of our attitudes? We could waste so much energy trying to figure out how the Virgin birth came about, or what the Angel Gabriel looked like, or what year this all happened in, or why Joseph should believe in his dreams, etc. We could so analyze Christmas that we end up missing the sheer magic of it. God loves us so much that He chose to become one of us, part of creation itself.

If I were God, I might consider creating a world, adding a few oceans and some high snow-capped mountains. I'd probably even place it in a universe with a nice bright sun and moon and some really bright stars. I'd probably add plants and animals and even some people too. I could see myself creating and really enjoying it. BUT THERE IS NO WAY I WOULD EVEN THINK ABOUT JOINING CREATION, BECOMING A PART OF IT! (if I were God). Lowering myself to become part of what I had made, no, if I were God, I would be a God who was clearly GODLIKE!

Christmas celebrates the fact that God loved us so much that He truly became one of us. If God, Who can do anything He wants, freely chooses to become part of the human race, isn't this truly amazing? If God has already done this for us, just imagine what He might be planning to do in the future!

Of all the greetings we receive at Christmas, the best one is still the one that Gabriel originally gave to Mary - think of it - THE LORD IS WITH YOU. And Christmas celebrates that the LORD IS WITH US TOO. That is certainly amazing and certainly worth celebrating. Don't let anything going on in the world or even in your own lives ever keep you from seeing the magic of Christmas or missing out on any of it. You're not coming here to try to figure it out; you've coming here to be amazed at the love God has for you. Whatever you do this week, don't miss the magic of Christmas!

God bless you!

❄ ❄ ❄

Christmas Eve and Christmas Day

25 December 2008

FIRST READING: Isaiah 9:1-6
PSALM: Psalm 96:1-3, 11-13
SECOND READING: Titus 3:11-14
GOSPEL: Luke 2:1-14

In the Gospel today, Joseph and Mary travel to Bethlehem for the census, and it is there in the City of David that Jesus is born.

A woman went to the Post Office to buy stamps for her Christmas card. **"What denomination?"** asked the clerk. **"Oh, good heavens! Have we come to this?"** said the woman, **"Well, give me 40 Catholic, 10 Baptist, 20 Lutheran, and 10 Presbyterian."**

A few days before Christmas, two young brothers were spending the night at the grandparents' home. When it was time to go to bed, and anxious to do the right thing, they both knelt down to say their prayers. Suddenly, the younger one began to pray in a very loud shouting voice: **"Dear Lord, please ask Santa Claus to bring me a Play-Station, a mountain bike, and a telescope."** His older brother leaned over and nudged him and said, **"Why are you shouting? God isn't deaf!"** And the younger brother replied, **"I know, but Grandma is!"**

In December 1903, after many attempts, the Wright Brothers were successful in getting their "flying machine" off the ground in Kitty Hawk, North Carolina. Thrilled, they telegraphed this message to their sister, Katherine, in Ohio: **"We have actually flown 120 feet. Will be home for Christmas."** Katherine hurried to the editor of the local newspaper and showed him the telegram. He glanced at it and said, **"How nice, the boys will be home for Christmas."** He totally missed the big news - man had flown, and the age of flight and space exploration had begun!

Is it possible that we have missed the **"big news"** about Christmas? Have we been so busy that the birth of Jesus Christ has been overshadowed by **"the holidays"**? Have we let ourselves or our families became **"P.A.C.E."** Catholics - **P.A.C.E.** - Catholics who show up at church for **PALMS** and **ASHES** and **CHRISTMAS** and **EASTER**.....and don't realize why any one of these days, and particularly CHRISTMAS, should overpower us with its importance?

Perhaps a little story will help.....There's a wonderful old story about a church in Holland. For many years, as long as anyone could remember, everyone entering the church would stop and bow in the direction of a whitewashed wall in the front of the church. Nobody knew why, but everyone had been doing it for so long that nobody ever questioned it. It was tradition. There was something fitting about it. It just felt right.

One day the parish decided to renovate the church. They began to strip the paint and white-wash off the old walls. And they discovered traces of a painting on the wall toward which everyone always bowed. They gently peeled off the paint, careful not to damage what was beneath it.

Slowly there emerged a beautiful, centuries old painting of Jesus Christ. Nobody in the parish was old enough to have ever seen it. It had been white-washed over for nearly two centuries. Yet, everyone had been bowing towards it, not knowing why, but sensing that there was a good reason for this reverence.

Gradually the story unfolded of how the painting came to be there and who had painted it. Now, when people entered the church and bowed to it, they knew why they were doing so.

I think there's a wonderful Christmas lesson in that little story. Everyone had been giving reverence to something whose meaning they could no longer see. They sensed there was something special about the wall, but the painting itself had been lost for a long time.

Isn't it interesting that most of Western culture pauses and still bows towards Christmas? Many may not know why, but we still put up a tree, string the lights, play the old Christmas carols, gather with our families and friends, and give each other gifts and cards. And more people still go to church on Christmas than on any other day of the year. Sure, some of this is driven by commercialism, and some of it is just habit. **But isn't some of it just like those people in that church in Holland in the story?** It is right to celebrate Christmas even if we don't always recognize the full meaning of what we are celebrating. And we should be happy that our world still makes a big deal out of Christmas.....even if it doesn't always realize the full reason behind the celebration.

No one loves Christmas more than I do. I love the cookies and cakes and even the fruitcakes (In case you were wondering what to do with yours!)

There is something **MAGICAL** about this whole season, something truly **WONDROUS**, something really **EXCITING**! You can feel it in the air! You can hear it in people's voices! You don't even have to be Catholic or Christian to get caught up in the excitement of Christmas. Everyone knows that there is something special.....kind of like knowing it was right to bow to that whitewashed wall in reverence.

But we know not only **WHAT** we are celebrating, but more importantly we know **WHO** we are celebrating at Christmas. Because when all is said and done, Christmas is about a **PERSON**, Jesus Christ. God chose to give us Himself. This is what we celebrate at Christmas. You and I know what is behind the whitewash on the wall. When we look at the manger, we know why we are celebrating Christmas.

Maybe we can help to strip away the paint and the whitewash for those in our families and among our friends who know that there is something right about Christmas, but haven't seen it clearly. The lights and the decorations will eventually be put away. The poinsettias will lose their leaves. The Christmas carols will be replaced by other music.... and eventually all the cookies and all the fruitcakes of the world will be eaten. **BUT JESUS WILL REMAIN WITH US! What a GIFT! What an incredible GIFT!**

If our greatest need had been information, God would have sent us an educator. If our greatest need had been technology, God would have sent us a scientist. If our greatest need had been money, God would have sent us an economist. If our greatest need had been pleasure, God would have sent us an entertainer. But our greatest need was forgiveness, love and salvation, so God sent us His Son, **JESUS**, as our **SAVIOR**.

We know **WHO** we are celebrating. Jesus is the **BEST GIFT** that God could possibly give us. God loves us so much that He gave us Himself. Now that's something to celebrate!

Merry Christmas!

The Holy Family of Jesus, Mary and Joseph

28 December 2009

FIRST READING: Sirach 3:2-7, 12-14
PSALM: Psalm 128:1-5
SECOND READING: Colossians 3:12-21
GOSPEL: Luke 2:22-40

In the Gospel today, Jesus is presented in the temple and then returns to Nazareth with Mary and Joseph where He grows up filled with God's wisdom.

Well, there is only one word for the Laughlin Report this week - FULL! Our worship on Christmas Eve and Christmas Day was full. In fact, we had over 100 MORE PEOPLE at Mass for Christmas this year than we did last Christmas. And that's all the more remarkable in our down-turned economy because there were actually fewer people in Laughlin this Christmas than last Christmas. Our poinsettias made the front of the church look so beautifully full too. And I think I will be opening Christmas cards for another few weeks. I don't think I have ever received so many cards with such beautiful notes in them. And the food.....well, let's just say that I feel really FULL! I couldn't begin to name them all, but there were some awesome homemade tamales, potato pie, chicken salad, rum balls, candy, cookies, and a wonderful concoction called "White Trash" made from white chocolate almond bark, pretzels, peanuts and some other great stuff. I've been on a sugar high since Thursday! We'll count the Christmas collection next week.....hopefully that will be FULL too! Thanks to everyone who celebrated Christmas with us. **It is awesome to be a priest here in Laughlin!**

One of the things I've noticed as a priest is that people sometimes come in to talk with me about their families.....and sometimes they're a bit embarrassed about what is going on in their families. Of course, I sometimes smile as I'm listening to them. Hey, I've got relatives too who are sometimes a bit strange! One of my relatives actually debated about telling her children that her husband (their father) had died. The children were all adults in their 40's, but she didn't want to upset them. Don't you think they would have noticed him missing from Thanksgiving Dinner? Or how about one of my relatives who decided to raise parakeets to make some extra money, so she ended up with a hundred of them in her bedroom. And then there was my relative who decided to raise chinchilla's in her house until she learned that you had to kill them to get their fur. By then, she had several dozen running around and didn't know what to do with them!

Of course, I'm not always a prize either! When I was a kid, I was once out with one of my aunts in Long Island. She went into a store and left me alone in the car. I had always wondered if a cigarette lighter stayed hot when she put it back into the little holder on the dashboard. So while she was gone, I took it out, pushed my index finger into it, and she came back to the car to find an hysterically-screaming kid with a burned finger bouncing around in the front seat!

After my Mom died, I was going through some of her things and I found an index card on which she had copied down a few sayings. One of them was: **"God gave us our relatives, thank God we can choose our friends."** I figure that must have been a bad day in our family! My other favorite saying is: **"Friends are God's apologies for giving us families."** So, in many ways, I like to count my friends as my family. In fact, I think all of us have some really awesome friends who really are just like family to us.

Today's feast of the Holy Family - Jesus, Mary and Joseph - reminds us that while we are all members of our human families, we are also all children of God. Some of us may be older or younger than others, and some of us are married or single, male or female, but as St. Paul reminds us in today's very powerful Second Reading: **WE ARE GOD'S CHOSEN ONES, HOLY AND BELOVED. THEREFORE WE MUST PUT ON HEARTFELT COMPASSION, KINDNESS, HUMILTY, GENTLENESS, AND PATIENCE.** We must learn to **FORGIVE** and to **LOVE** and to be **THANKFUL** precisely because of our relationship with God. He has chosen us to be part of His family, and to be His friends.

But because we are also members of our human families and our human communities, we have all the ups and downs, all the joys and sorrows, all the good things and bad things, all the opportunities and limitations of any family or community. As God's chosen ones, we **TRY** to be forgiving, we **TRY** to be thankful, we **TRY** to be patient, we **TRY** to bear with one another, and we **TRY** to love one another. We know that this is what we are supposed to do. Some days we do it better than others. Other days, it takes all that we have just to keep from criminal assault on our neighbor, co-worker, friend or spouse!

Eventually we all learn that we can't do it on our own, we need God's help not only to assist us in becoming our best selves, but sometimes just in order to keep us from acting like our worst selves. May the example of Jesus, Mary and Joseph inspire us in the coming year to grow into the family members of God's family and our human families that God calls us to be.

If even Jesus could advance in wisdom and age and favor, you and I can certainly try to do so too. And the new year is a great time to learn to treat family members and friends better than ever before.

God bless you!

The Blessed Virgin Mary, Mother of God

1 January 2009

FIRST READING: Numbers 6:22-27
PSALM: Psalm 67:2-3, 5-6, 8
SECOND READING: Galatians 4:4-7
GOSPEL: Luke 2: 16-21

In the Gospel today, the shepherds go in haste to see the Baby Jesus in Bethlehem while Mary keeps all of this within her heart reflecting upon it.

There's a wonderful old story that has made the rounds many times. As we come to the start of a brand new year, I think that this old story might point us in the right direction.

An old man sat on a park bench each morning feeding the birds and the squirrels. No matter what the weather, he was always there, and he was always smiling. He always seemed to dress pretty much the same - an old coat in winter, a faded shirt in summer. But he was always smiling and he always seemed happy.

A young businessman used to pass by each day on his way to work. He was always in a rush, always looking frazzled. He noticed the old man on the bench, but he was always too much in a rush to stop. But more and more, the sight of the old man on the bench bothered him. What was he smiling about? What was he happy about? He seemed to have so little. What was wrong with him?

One day, the young frazzled businessman couldn't stand it anymore. He stopped and he looked the old man right in the eye as he said: **"What are you smiling about? What are you so happy about? You have nothing. You sit here every day feeding birds and squirrels. What can you be so happy about?"**

The old man looked him right back in the eye and without missing a beat said: **"Sonny, when I get up in the morning, I figure I have two choices - I can choose to be miserable or I can choose to be happy. I'm not stupid, Sonny! I choose to be happy!"**

Every new year, many of us make resolutions. We resolve to lose weight. We resolve to spend more time with our families. We resolve to be more generous to charity. All of these are good things, but this year I would like to suggest one New Year's resolution which we may not have thought about making in past years. This new year, resolve to be happy!

We can't control much of what life hands us. Some of it is really great and some of it is really awful and hard to swallow. But nothing happens to any of us that is outside of God's love and God's concern. And if the fact that God, the Almighty Creator of the universe and everything in it, loves you and is concerned about you doesn't make you feel even a little happy, then I don't know anything that ever will.

My suggestion as we enter 2009 - remember the wisdom of that wise old man: **"Sonny, when I get up in the morning, I figure I have two choices - I can choose to be miserable or I can choose to be happy! I'm not stupid, Sonny! I choose to be happy!"**

God bless you!

Father Charlie and his amazing family!
Eddie, Fr. Charlie, Andy and Michael

The Epiphany of the Lord

4 January 2009

FIRST READING: Isaiah 60:1-6
PSALM: Psalm 72:2, 7-8, 10-13
SECOND READING: Ephesians 3:2-3a, 5-6
GOSPEL: Matthew 2:1-12

In the Gospel today, the wise men follow a star, and it leads them right to Jesus.

On New Year's Day, it was 65 degrees and sunny in Laughlin while in New Jersey, it was 13 degrees, snowing and the wind-chill factor was below zero! Golly, I'm glad to be here in Laughlin! And this new year, 2009, we'll mark the 100th anniversary of Clark County, Nevada, on July 1st. That will give us something extra to celebrate this summer. And speaking of celebrating, last weekend, I told you how full I was feeling with all the additional Christmas foods that were given to me. I'm going to be eating fruitcake almost into the summer! And I'm still thrilled that we had over 1500 people attend Christmas Mass with us. I don't usually like to talk about money, but now I have to tell you that we counted our Christmas collection and we had more than **DOUBLE** the amount collected last Christmas! In fact, so far the Christmas collection for this year amounts to $13,562.50.....and there's still more to be counted! This is by far the largest Christmas collection in the history of our church here in Laughlin. So our collection plates were as full on Christmas as my stomach was! Thank you! Thank you! Thank you! For food, faith, friendliness and finances, you are the best!

On New Year's Eve and New Year's Day, besides celebrating Mass and eating lots of fruitcake and cookies, I also got to do something that I always enjoy. The SciFi Channel was featured a **TWILIGHT ZONE MARATHON** of 68 episodes spread out over 48 hours! And I love the old black and white Twilight Zone shows! The series ran from 1959 until 1964 with over 150 episodes. I watched a lot of them! And this week, I even got to see three episodes that I had never seen before! And I got to see a number of my very favorite episodes. I especially like the one called **TO SERVE MAN** which involves creatures from another planet visiting earth with seemingly good motives.....until their book - **TO SERVE MAN** - is translated and it is discovered that it is actually a cookbook! And even though I had seen many of these episodes many times before, I still learned new things about them and I still found it remarkable that so many of the episodes were very religious in nature and involved man's search for meaning and fulfillment. In fact, seeing them again was perhaps even better than seeing them for the first time. I guess we do see things and hear things differently based on our life experiences. I was just a kid when I first saw the Twilight Zone. Now 50 years later, the shows are still impressive and maybe have a few more layers of meaning that I had never seen before.

I guess the same thing might pretty much describe our approach to the Scriptures. Today's Gospel passage from St. Matthew about the Magi is a really familiar one, and yet each year we hear it a little differently. Maybe some years we concentrate on their faithfulness in following that star, while other years we think about their generosity in offering gifts. And then again, we might be thinking about the reactions of Joseph and Mary to having such visitors in their home. We might even wonder about the details of their journey. But it is good to hear the story again and to reflect upon it.

Perhaps you have heard of a piece of writing called **DESIDERATA**, written by Max Ehrmann over 80 years ago in 1927 out in Terre Haute, Indiana. It's one of my absolute favorite pieces of literature and I think it is worth taking the time to read it aloud as we journey into this new year 2009. I know we may have heard it before, but since hearing it, we've had time to experience more of life's lessons in our families, in our church, in our nation, and in our world. It's good for us to hear it again, and I offer it as an insight into the new year for each one of us. I think it is one of the most beautiful and most powerful pieces of literature I have ever come across. Listen carefully to what it is saying to you right now:

DESIDERATA - THINGS TO BE DESIRED

Go placidly amid the noise and the haste, and remember what peace there may be in silence. As far as possible without surrender be on good terms with all persons. Speak your truth quietly and clearly; and listen to others, even to the dull and the ignorant; they too have their story. Avoid loud and aggressive persons, they are vexations to the spirit.

If you compare yourself with others, you may become vain or bitter; for always there will be greater and lesser persons than yourself. Enjoy your achievements as well as your plans. Keep interested in your own career, however humble; it is a real possession in the changing fortunes of time.

Exercise caution in your business affairs, for the world is full of trickery. But let not this blind you to what virtue there is; many persons strive for high ideals, and everywhere life is full of heroism. Be yourself. Especially do not feign affection. Neither be cynical about love; for in the face of all aridity and disenchantment, it was as perennial as the grass. Take kindly the counsel of the years, gracefully surrendering the things of youth.

Nurture strength of spirit to shield you in sudden misfortune. But do not distress yourself with dark imaginings. Many fears are born of fatigue and loneliness. Beyond a wholesome discipline, be gentle with yourself. You are a child of the universe, no less than the trees and the stars; you have a right to be here. And whether or not it is clear to you, no doubt the universe is unfolding as it should.
Therefore, be at peace with God, whatever you conceive Him to be. And whatever your labors and aspirations in the noisy confusion of life, keep peace in your soul. With all its sham, drudgery and broken dreams; it is still a beautiful world. Be cheerful. Strive to be happy.

As we begin this new year 2009, we all have hopes and dreams, goals and expectations for the new year. Some of them are like stars, they seem so distant, so unreachable. Remember the wise men. They followed a star and it led them right to Jesus. For this new year, follow the best of your hopes and dreams, keep looking to God for guidance, find some words of truth and make them your own. And we too will be led right to Jesus. And there is no other place we should rather be in this new year. Stick close to the Lord, and you can't go wrong!

God bless you, and have a Happy New Year in 2009!

Eddie, Fr. Charlie, and Michael

❖ ❖ ❖

The Baptism of the Lord

11 January 2009

FIRST READING: Isaiah 55:1-11
PSALM: Isaiah 12:2-3, 4-6
SECOND READING: 1 John 5:1-9
GOSPEL: Mark 1:7-11

In the Gospel today, Jesus is baptized by John in the Jordan River, and the Holy Spirit descends upon Him in the form of a dove.

Another great week in Laughlin! Have you ever noticed how beautiful the mountains and the big blue sky look when you're driving up Bruce Woodbury Drive? I keep wanting to stop and take pictures! Tourists travel hundreds of miles to see what I get to see every day! My friends in New Jersey have started referring to Laughlin as "Paradise" when they write or call me because I've told them so much about it. I intend to spend eternity in the real Paradise, but until then, Laughlin comes pretty close! I'm still enjoying the remnants of Christmas cookies and the remaining fruitcakes. Somehow I managed to have eggplant parmegiana (which I love!) three times this week. And another friend from New York City came out to visit. He would never cross the Hudson River to see me when I lived in New Jersey, but he flew to Nevada last week. **I guess you never really know how many friends you have until you have a guest room in Paradise!**

Oh, and I learned something new with the crowds that were in Laughlin over Christmas and New Year's. I had to park my car farther out in the parking lots when I came over to the casinos and I would sometimes have trouble finding it. So I would push on the little electric key thing to make the car headlights blink. The only problem is that sometimes the car was too far away for it to work. Then one of my friends told me that if you hold the device up to your chin, it more than doubles the distance the signal travels. Kind of like it uses your head as an antenna! Just thought I'd share that really useful piece of advice. It really works! **Just one more thing I like about being a priest here in Paradise..... people feed more and people tell me really useful things!**

One of the other things I like about being a priest is baptizing babies. I've baptized almost 600 babies! And these ceremonies are always exciting. You never know what the baby will do when suddenly he/she is confronted with a strange man pouring cool water over his/her head. But as much as I love the ceremony itself, I love the preparation time with first-time parents even more. For parents, as well as for their children, Baptism is often a new beginning of Faith. Becoming a mother and a father sometimes brings the couple back to practicing the Faith they are asking to be given to their child. It does make sense...after all, why would you want to have your child baptized into a Faith that you yourself don't bother to practice?

Besides the important theology, there are two things that I usually point out to the parents. The first is to make certain that whomever is holding the baby for the Baptism know what he/she is doing! Babies can make some strange and sudden movements when hit with water! As one father put it, **"My son became a screaming, quivering mass of human flesh!"** Sometimes Godparents are not used to the possible movements that a baby might make. As for me, I have only one baby-holding position. I can expand it or make it smaller, but I can't change it! I guess it's fortunate that I became a priest!

The other point that I make strongly with the parents is the beauty of the blessing of the baptismal water. We take plain Laughlin tap water and bless it with a lengthy blessing that recalls a number of occasions when God has used water in the past to achieve some purpose or miracle. I usually ask the parents what examples of this they might recall hearing about in the Bible. Sometimes I have to prod them to remember what they have heard. I had one class where a parents remembered Jesus washing the Apostles' feet with water on Holy Thursday at the Last Supper. I said, "Great! Now think of something in the Bible with more water!" So someone remembered Jesus turning gallons of water into wine at the wedding feast at Cana. I said, "Think of more water!".....and someone remembered Jesus' own Baptism in the Jordan River by St. John the Baptist (which we commemorate today). And then I said, "Think of even more water!".....and someone remembered Moses leading the Israelites across the Red Sea out of slavery into freedom. I was pleased, and then I said, "You're missing one really big event with a whole lot more water!" But no one got it. Finally I gave them a hint, "BIG BOAT!" And then they remembered Noah and the ark when God cleansed the whole earth with water.

Why make such a big thing about a blessing of water for Baptism? Because at every Baptism Jesus continues to work wonders with water. It is no less a miracle than the crossing of the Red Sea, or the changing of water into wine, or the cleansing of the whole earth at the time of Noah, that God Himself would bring creatures like us into His kingdom for all eternity. But that is in fact what Baptism does. When we are baptized, we begin the process by which we will develop in the Catholic Faith and eventually, God willing, inherit eternal life with God. Each Baptism is the beginning of an eternal miracle. And it is a step towards eternity in the real Paradise!

All of us who have been baptized have been brought into a relationship with God that will last for all eternity. As we celebrate today the Baptism of Jesus, I just thought it would be good to remind you how fortunate we are to have been baptized. Isaiah puts it very well in today's First Reading: "I, the Lord, have called you; I have grasped you by the hand." Just think of that image for a moment.....you and I are walking hand-in-hand with God! Doesn't that make you feel really secure? When things get really tough as they sometimes do in life, you can reach out and God's hand will be there to steady you and to support you.

As we continue our journey through life, may we never forget how close God has chosen to be to us. May we keep our hands safely in His throughout our lives. What began at our Baptism goes on into eternity. **How fortunate we are to be holding hands with God!**

God bless you!

Our beautiful St. Joseph Table set for March 19th.

2nd Sunday in Ordinary Time - "B"

18 January 2009

FIRST READING: 1 Samuel 3:3b-10, 19
PSALM: Psalm 40:2, 4, 7-10
SECOND READING: 1 Corinthians 6:13c-15a, 17-20
GOSPEL: John 1:35-42

In the Gospel today, Jesus calls His Apostles to follow Him, and in the Book of Samuel we are told to listen to the Lord calling each one of us.

Ah, another week in Paradise (also known as Laughlin!) There was some more garlic mashed potatoes and some homemade cinnamon buns, and a pasta served with homemade chunky tomato sauce laced with good red wine! And homemade guacamole spiked with fresh lime juice! And the Steelers' fans were active this week.....emailing me pictures of dead Ravens on the road, and warning me not to wear anything purple this weekend! (They're just lucky that we're not in Lent....then I'd be in purple vestments with Steelers' socks!). And, of course, now there are two other birds to consider - the Cardinals and the Eagles. If I tried to wear something for every team, I'd be looking mighty strange! I've never been much of a football fan, but I may have to actually start watching some of these games! My friend, Flash, was in Vegas this past week. I usually see him and Crazy Tattooed Tony up in Massachusetts. I've got to get a cool name for myself! And Flash is friends with David Copperfield so I got to see David's show at the MGM in Vegas, and then hang out with him backstage after the show. While Flash and I were having dinner after the show, David called and invite us to meet him for a private movie screening at 2:00 AM. But by then, I needed some sleep so I decided to call it a night and go to bed. So now I can actually say that I turned down an invitation from David Copperfield! It was another amazing week in Paradise!

There's a wonderful old story about a priest who felt called to help his parishioners prepare for death. He thought about it and prayed about it and finally decided that he needed to preach about it. So he came up with a powerful opening line for his sermon. He walked to the pulpit, adjusted the mike, looked out at the people in the congregation, and said: **"Everyone in this parish will someday die!"** He paused to let it sink in, and then noticed an old man smiling in the first row. The priest thought that the old man hadn't heard him, so he decided to start his sermon again. He adjusted the mike, and spoke a little louder as he said: **"Everyone in this parish will someday die!"** And as he looked at the old man, he saw that the old man was chuckling! Well, this really bothered the priest so he was sure the old man hadn't heard him about so serious a topic. So, once again, he began his sermon, this time staring at the old man and shouting his opening line into the microphone: **"Everyone in this parish will some-day die!"** And now the old man was laughing out loud! So the priest left the pulpit, ran up to the old man, grabbed him by the collar, shook him, and said: **"What are you laughing at?"** And the old man replied: **"I'm not from this parish."**

There's a truth to every story. Aren't we all sometimes like that old man when we come to church? Don't we sometimes think that the Scriptures and the sermon are intended for someone else? **They** should shape up! **They** should do what's right! **They** need to reform their lives! Today's First Reading from the Book of Samuel reminds us that God is calling each one of us by name. Not just the person next to you or in front of you, but **YOU**! And our response should be to listen to what the Lord is calling us to do. **"Speak, Lord, for your servant is listening."**

And our Second Reading from St. Paul's Letter to the Corinthians reminds us that our bodies are members of Christ's Body. Our bodies are Temples of God. Therefore, we have to resist immorality. We have to try to live holy and decent lives. That means each one of us, you and me.

And in today's Gospel from St. John, we are being called to follow Jesus, and to share Him with others. No one can take our place.

The big lesson that we should take home with us today is that whenever we hear the Scriptures, whenever we hear the sermon, whenever we spend time in prayer, we should be listening to what God is trying to say to us. He's not just talking to our neighbors. He's talking to us. And we need to be listening so we don't miss out on hearing what he wants us to do. Sure we can turn down an invitation from David Copperfield, but we should never turn down an invitation from God. Like Samuel, we need to be listening.

God bless you!

3rd Sunday in Ordinary Time - "B"

25 January 2009

FIRST READING: Jonah 3:1-5, 10
PSALM: Psalm 25:4-9
SECOND READING: 1 Corinthians 7:29-31
GOSPEL: Mark 1:14-20

In the Gospel today, Jesus teaches that the Kingdom of God is at hand, and in the Book of Jonah we see an important lesson about faith and forgiveness.

Once a year, the Diocese of Las Vegas has a Clergy Education Week. So this past week, I was away in San Bernardino with the other priests of the diocese. The topic was an update on the new translations of the readings and the Roman Missal which will likely be in use in another few years. Some of the presentations on the translations of various texts were really dull! And some of the suggested new translations are really tongue-twisters. But we'll handle that when the time comes. But the best part of the week was getting to spend some time with the other priests of the diocese. Had dinner one night with Father John McShane, the first priest assigned to Laughlin, so you were very much in our thoughts and conversation. It was also kind of cool to hang out with the bishop and discover that he enjoys eating as much as I do! Speaking of eating, I even got taken out to dinner one night in San Bernardino by a couple who lives there but who have come to Mass at the Riverside frequently when they visit Laughlin. So, because of Laughlin, I even get fed when I'm out of town! **(This place is AWESOME!)** Meanwhile back here in Laughlin, I've got a turkey pot pie and some remaining turkey chili to enjoy. And one of my friends even found a lime cactus beer for me to try. **"Always something new, always something fun**!" - maybe that's another good slogan for Laughlin.

Oh, and I was asked last week by a regular Mass attendee, if I was getting paid by the Laughlin Visitors Center for my comments on Laughlin. No, I guess my comments fall under the category of "free advertising" for a place I really love. Just wait until Biker Week in April! I'm sure I'll find some really interesting things to say then!

Somewhere along the way, most of us have probably heard a radio commentator named Paul Harvey. He has a very unique style of telling the news, and many of you are already thinking about his trademark line: **"AND NOW, THE REST OF THE STORY!"** Well, I'd like to steal that line from Paul Harvey and tell you the "rest of the story" about today's First Reading from the Book of Jonah.

We join the story today in Chapter Three - what happened, you might wonder, in the two previous chapters? SOMETHING ABOUT A WHALE...but more than that! In Chapter One, God asks Jonah to do exactly the same thing that He asks in Chapter Three: **"Go to Ninevah and announce My message!"** But in

Chapter One, Jonah says **"NO!"** and sets off in the opposite direction seeking to get as far away from God as possible. He is unsuccessful because, as we all know, GOD IS EVERYWHERE. And so, when Jonah is thrown off a pagan ship during a fierce storm, God is there and He "rescues" Jonah in a way. Jonah is swallowed whole by a huge fish. (The story doesn't actually say "WHALE", but it helps us to visualize a WHALE even though a WHALE technically is not a FISH anyway! But if we thought that Jonah had been swallowed by a barracuda or a shark or a guppie, the logistics would become really difficult!)

Fortunately, Jonah isn't digested by the whale, but he does get some very private time to think over his response to God and he does pray to the Lord. In fact, his prayer changes his attitude and when the whale spits him out onto a beach, and God asks him again about going to Ninevah, Jonah immediately responds **"YES!"**...and that is where we find him in today's First Reading.

But what happens next? After Chapter Three? Is Jonah happy about his success? No way! Now he's angry at God because God is merciful. You see, Jonah hated the Ninevites and really wanted God to punish them because they were the enemies of his people (the Israelites). If God can forgive even the people of Ninevah (whom Israel hated), then God could forgive ANYONE! The story ends with God very patiently trying to show Jonah the value of being kind and merciful. And this is the rest of the story!

Now, if the past few minutes have reminded you of a classroom lecture instead of a sermon, GOOD! That was my plan! Today we begin CATHOLIC SCHOOLS WEEK, and many of us are the products of a Catholic School education. Even though we don't have a Catholic School here in Laughlin, every time we come to Mass, we're learning something about God and His Church. So our time here is not just a worship experience, it's a learning experience.

And, I guess I really should give you a homework assignment since I gave you a classroom lecture today.....

This week, pull out your Bible (dust it off, if necessary!). For those of you staying in one of Laughlin's awesome resorts, there should be one conveniently located in the night table drawer. Then read the whole BOOK OF JONAH. It's only about 2 pages long. We can all learn a lot from him.

The people of Ninevah got 40 days, and they changed their ways, and they were saved. I don't know how smart the average Ninevite was, but apparently he was smart enough to realize that he only had a limited amount of time to do something about his relationship with Almighty God. I hope that each one of us here today is at least as smart as the average Ninevite!

Oh, by the way, just a little bit of trivia.....ancient Ninevah was located in modern-day Iraq, not too far from the present site of Baghdad. Perhaps reading the story of Jonah this week when world attention is looking at that region might be a good way for us to prayerfully approach the world situation.

And that, my friends, is "the rest of the story!"

God bless you!

4th Sunday in Ordinary Time - "B"

1 February 2009

FIRST READING: Deuteronomy 18:15-20
PSALM: Psalm 95:1-2, 6-9
SECOND READING: 1 Corinthians 7:32-35
GOSPEL: Mark 1:21-28

In the Gospel today, Jesus teaches with real authority which gives Him real power as God in this world.

Ah, another incredible week in Paradise! There were plenty of cakes and pies, a Boston cream pie, home chop suey, cheddar cheese from Wisconsin, some Cinnabons, and an awesome apple crumb dessert pizza! 98 people came with me to see Mac King's Comedy Magic Show in Las Vegas. Watch your bulletins for more trips in the coming months. And my buddy Michael started to teach me about being "cool" and using "Facebook" like a pro! I'll probably never be "cool", but "Facebook" is a lot of fun. He's an incurable Steelers' fan, so I decided to look up some comments about football when it was just a new game. Here's what I found.....

In 1531, the Puritan preacher, Thomas Eliot, argued that football caused "beastly fury and extreme violence." In 1572, the Bishop of Rochester demanded a new campaign to suppress this "evil game." In 1583, Philip Stubbs wrote that: "Football playing and other devilish pastimes withdraweth us from

Godliness, either upon the Sabbath or any other day." Stubbs was also concerned about the injuries that were taking place: "sometimes their necks are broken, sometimes their backs, sometimes their legs, sometimes their arms, sometimes one part is thrust out of joint, sometimes the noses gush out with blood. Football encourages envy and hatred, sometimes fighting, murder and a great loss of blood." But it is possible to relate football to church. Just check out Page 7 of this week's parish bulletin.

And just for the record.....I'm wearing Steelers' socks. No Cardinals' fans have given me anything red to wear. Enough said. I hope it's a great game! Lot of fun for everyone. And may the best team win!

Shortly before I came out to Laughlin, I was visiting a young baby in a hospital in New Jersey, and I was talking with her father (Dino) in the pediatric ICU. The doctor came in and after examining the baby started to talk to Dino about her and then pointed to me while asking Dino "Is this your Dad?" And he responded, "No, he's just my Father." I've got to dye this hair!

This week marks the 23rd anniversary of the explosion of the Space Shuttle Challenger back in 1986. It was one of those pivotal moments in time when most of us of a certain age can vividly remember exactly where we were when it happened. For years to come, it will be passed down to the younger members of our families what it was like to see that explosion on live TV. And yet, even with our explanations, there is still no real way for them to know exactly what it felt like to actually watch it happen, that sinking feeling when you knew it was over.

On my 58th birthday a few years ago, I was out in Fort Atkinson, Wisconsin. I spent the day at the Fireside Dinner Theater where they were doing a revue show called "The Fabulous 50's". A buddy of mine, Rico, was in the show. He's in his 30's, but the rest of the cast are mainly 20-21 year olds. I met the cast before the afternoon show, then saw the two and a half hour show which was awesome! Then I had dinner with the cast before seeing the evening show. In fact, I enjoyed the dinner time even more than the shows themselves. The cast quickly realized that I had actually lived through the 1950's, so I became this kind of ancient guru for them! They knew all the songs and slang and celebrities and dances from the 1950's, but they didn't know them from personal experience. So I got questions like:

"What's a Nash Rambler? And why do the audiences laugh at that song about the little Nash Rambler beating a Cadillac in a race? You know the one...BEEP, BEEP, THE HORN GOES BEEP, BEEP, BEEP!"

"What's chantilly lace?"

"Did they really have dances called the MASHED POTATO, the STROLL, and the PEPPERMINT TWIST?"

"Did the girls really wear pink skirts with black poodles on them?"

"What's a 45 record?.....What's a record player?"

"Did everyone really watch the Milton Berle Show and the Ed Sullivan Show?"

And you should have seen their looks when I told them about a show called "Winkie Dink" and the "John Nagy Art Show" and how we would buy sheets of thin plastic that would stick to our black and white TV screens by static cling so we could draw on them during those shows! I remember getting yelled at once when I was drawing on the TV screen with my crayons, but had forgotten to put on the plastic sheet!

Hey, we didn't have "GAMEBOY" and "NINTENDO" and "Wii"....those plastic sheets were our interactive video games!

And, once I was talking to the cast and crew of a high school production of the play "Miss Saigon." The story is set in the 1970's and concerns the last days and aftermath of the Vietnam War. Again, I was the old guru telling these kids about what it was like to live in America during that tumultuous time. They knew the words, they knew the story, but it just wasn't real for them because it wasn't their own experience.

There is something about being there and living through these important events. And sometimes it is hard to convey what the experiences really had been like. But hearing about them from an eyewitness really makes a big difference.

So, what's the point of these rambling remembrances from me? Sure, they all serve to make me feel incredibly old! But besides that, they also served to remind all of us of the importance of eyewitness accounts, of the testimony of those who were really there. Like in today's Gospel where Mark recounts Jesus teaching with authority in the synagogue at Capernaum and driving out an unclean spirit, a demon. It's not just a nice story from a past age. It's a lesson being taught to us by someone who lived through it. That, after all, is one of the reasons why the Scripture readings are so important in our Masses and in our Catholic education programs. They bring us together with those who have lived through the events.

It's good for all of us to remember that we all have a role in communicating our Catholic Faith to the next generation. We all have experiences of our Catholic Faith to share as eyewitnesses to what it means to be a man or a woman of Faith. Parents who bring their children to church teach by their words as well as by their example. Grandparents who share stories of their youth remind grandchildren that life is bigger than their own little worlds and neighborhoods.

We are all eyewitnesses to the truth of our Catholic Faith and what it means to live as Catholics. We need to pass that on as only we can do. We pray this week that we will do it well, that we will be eye-witnesses to the truth of our lived Catholic Faith. The older we get, the more we've experienced, the more we have to share. That's true about life, and that's true about our Catholic Faith.

God bless you!

5th Sunday in Ordinary Time - "B"

8 February 2009

FIRST READING: Job 7:1-4, 6-7
PSALM: Psalm 147:1-6
SECOND READING: 1 Corinthians 9:16-19, 22-23
GOSPEL: Mark 1:29-39

In the Gospel today, Jesus drives out many demons, and in the Reading from the Book of Job, we explore the mystery of evil coexisting with good in the world.

Another week in the warm paradise of Laughlin. Somehow it feels even better knowing that New Jersey is still in the deep freeze! I've been feasting on some lemon-iced coconut cake, lemon poppyseed muffins, plenty of cookies, homemade brownies, homemade hot peppers, and a wonderful arab dinner. The family from Bethlehem who sold the olivewood products here around Christmas invited me to their home in Las Vegas for dinner. They were going to make lamb or goat, but I asked if we could have a vegetarian dinner so we had zucchini stuffed with rice and vegetables, hummus, sesame seed bread, and babakanoush! Then they brought out a bottle of Arac. It's like a 50 proof liquorice liquor! I sipped a tiny glass for about an hour! **Again, because I'm in Laughlin, I got invited out to eat in Vegas! What a great life! I love this place!**

And last Sunday, the guy who plays Frank Sinatra in the Rat Pack Show was at Mass with us. After Mass, he and I got talking and he asked if I had seen the Rat Pack Show. I told him I had seen it on the very first night, and I said it was a really good show. He told me, "Yours was too!" and then he invited me to see his show up in Vegas. And I got to hang out with my Vegas buddies Michael and Eddie until 3:00 AM on Wednesday night. They had auditioned for a job working poolside as bartender/entertainers at the MGM and had to stand around for two hours in an air-conditioned showroom in just swim trunks waiting to be interviewed. I jokingly had said I wouldn't go along with them because I didn't want to take the job away from them! But they both very seriously said, **"Charlie, if they saw you in swim trunks, they would have asked you to put your clothing back on!"** Now that was really depressing!

Speaking of depressing...Oh gosh, today's first reading from the Book of Job is really depressing! "Man's life on earth is a drudgery"....."I have been assigned months of misery."....."the night drags on"....."my days come to an end without hope".....I shall not see happiness again." Certainly not something to read when you're having a down day! Today's first reading from the Book of Job is definitely not something you want to read when you're having a bad day! Rather than leave you thinking such depressing thoughts, let me just say a few words about the whole Book of Job. I'm not going to attempt to explain it all, but I'd like to highlight some of its teachings!

The Book of Job is part of the Wisdom Literature in the Bible's Old Testament. It confronts the mystery of evil in the world. It asks the question over and over again that many of us have pondered: "Why do good people suffer?" And much as we'd like God to give us an answer, the only answer we get from the Book of Job is basically: "Don't ask!"

Job loses just about everything...his children, his wealth, his property, his health. From being a rich and respected citizen with everything going his way, Job becomes a poor man, covered with sores, and sitting on an ash heap in poverty and pain.

But even though Job questions God, Job never gives up on God. He knows God is there, he just wants to understand what is going on in his life. And after Job questions God, God then questions Job in a scene that is among the most memorable in all the Scriptures. "Where were you when I created the heavens?", God asks. "Were you there when I made the mountains or the animals or when I created the rain or the sun or the stars?...Tell me, if you are so wise, how I devised the planets and set up the sun." And Job eventually responds: "I put my hand over my mouth. I cannot answer. I am speechless before You."

At the very end of the Book of Job, Job's wealth and good fortune and good health are restored and multiplied. He even begets more children as a sign of God's favor. But Job has learned a very important lesson: no matter what happens, we are answerable to God, but God is never answerable to us. God doesn't have to explain His actions or His plans to us. We are creatures. God is the Almighty Creator.

So does the Bible answer the question about suffering? In a way, yes, it does. The Book of Job tells us that somehow suffering - mental and physical - is part of the human experience. And while God promises to be with us no matter what happens, God is never in the position of having to explain Himself to us.

I rather doubt that any of us will ever have to endure the sufferings of Job, but I hope we can cultivate the patience and the wisdom of Job. I hope we can come to the point in our lives where we really do believe that God knows what He is doing, and that we can accept that as enough of an answer for us no matter what is going on around us in our own little world or in the big world around us. You and I are only creatures, standing before God the Almighty Creator, speechless sometimes at His power and greatness, but always trusting in His goodness and mercy.

God bless you!

6th Sunday in Ordinary Time - "B"

15 February 2009

FIRST READING: Leviticus 13:1-2, 44-46
PSALM: Psalm 32:1-2, 5, 11
SECOND READING: 1 Corinthians 10:31 - 11:1
GOSPEL: Mark 1:40-45

In the Gospel today, Jesus cures a leper using His Divine power, and in the Reading from St. Paul's Letter to the Corinthians, we are asked to imitate Paul who is imitating Jesus.

Another amazing week in Paradise! The weather is sure better than back in New Jersey in the winter! And the food here is spectacular! Had an awesome Southwest salad (corn, peppers, mayo, and crumbled corn chips), lime/butter marinated chicken, green bean casserole, cherry pie, ravioli, spinach/mushroom scrambled eggs, tomato soup. Ah, it's going to be so hard in Lent to say "NO" to all those goodies! But there's still a week and a half until the fasting starts, so I'm making the most of it!

Got out to my monthly lunch with Father Peter from across the river. We're working our way through all the restaurants in Laughlin and Bullhead City, alternating from his side of the river to mine. Whenever any of our parishioners see us, we usually smile and say, "Oh, we were just talking about you!" Just a little clergy humor...as we watch their expressions!

And the bargains here are amazing! I needed my On-Star antenna repaired on my Saturn. Checked up in Vegas and it would cost $400.00 there. Found a place here that will do it for less than half that. I love this place!

Went shopping with two of my entertainer friends in Vegas. They wanted me to imitate them. So they told me that the right pair of tight jeans, slick stub-pointed shoes, and a chain hanging from the waist would make anyone look "cool" and "in"! We sure disproved that myth! After some encounters with Vegas upscale shops (and me gagging on the thought of jeans that cost over $300.00!), they decided that I'd just never be cool! The overweight elderly biker look just wasn't my style! Besides, I don't even think they make cool jeans in my size! But it was fun playing around with the idea!

I'm still having fun on Facebook and keeping up with my friends through emails. But there was been so much email and news traffic to read lately that it is hard to get to all of it, and still pretend that I really do work.

I recall a speed-reading course I took many years ago that recommended trying to find the one significant sentence in each paragraph and remembering that as the key to remembering and digesting the whole paragraph. I thought I would apply that idea to today's Second Reading from the First Letter of St. Paul to the Corinthians. St. Paul writes boldly: **"Be imitators of me, as I am of Christ."**

Let's just think about that single sentence for a few moments today. How many of us could dare to hold ourselves up as an example for others to imitate in everything? Would we really want out children, our spouses, our friends and neighbors to think and act the way we do in all things? Maybe in some areas of our lives, but in everything?

St. Paul writes that he tries to do everything for the glory of God and that he is an imitator of Christ. Now there's the key to a holy Christian life if I ever saw one! We need to think before we speak, we need to think before we act. And what do we need to think about? We need to think about whether what we are about to say or do is actually going to be said or done for the glory of God and in imitation of Jesus Christ.

I suggest simply that some things would never be said or done if people who profess to be Catholic Christians actually applied their religious beliefs to their daily lives. And there would probably be an equally large number of things that WOULD ACTU-ALLY be said or done if people actually thought about what their religious beliefs should motivate them to do in their daily lives.

St. Paul wanted to imitate Christ, and to do it so well and so consistently that he could boldly ask others to follow his example. This week, as we consider St. Paul's words, maybe we could try to do the same. Our world at large and our little world of family and friends could certainly use the benefit of a few good examples to imitate. We could be those examples. In fact, we should be those examples. With St. Paul, we should be able to say: "Be imitators of me, as I am of Christ." At the very least, it certainly wouldn't hurt to try!

God bless you!

7th Sunday in Ordinary Time - "B"

22 February 2009

FIRST READING: Isaiah 43:18-19, 21-22, 24b-25
PSALM: Psalm 41:2-5, 13-14
SECOND READING: 2 Corinthians 1:18-22
GOSPEL: Mark 2:1-12

In the Gospel today, Jesus cures a paralyzed man because of the faith shown by the man's friends.

What an incredible week! Last weekend, there was a great homemade Polish dinner for Valentine's Day! Nothing says love like pyrogi stuffed with cheese or sauerkraut or potatoes! And golumpke made with turkey, and fruit-stuffed pyrogi for dessert along with poppyseed cake and chrischiki! And lots of leftovers came home with me! And then there was a homemade pineapple upside down cake, and lime squares!

And my friend Michael celebrated his 39th birthday up in Vegas by inviting some of his East Coast friends. Since we share some of the same friends over the years and we moved out to Nevada at about the same time, it was like this really awesome reunion for all of us! From late on Tuesday until Friday morning, we had a blast! I got to sleep one morning at 5:00 AM! And the other nights were darn close to that too! I can't tell you everything - you know that "What happens in Vegas, stays in Vegas" - thing!

I finally drank a full bottle of beer! I've never liked beer, but one of the guys introduced me to something called Blue Moon which has an orange taste, and it was actually quite good! I learned to play three-card poker and I won $60.00! I played my Zeus penny slot and I won $342.00 at 4:30 AM on morning! One day we went hiking and rock climbing at Red Rock Canyon (and I survived!). I'm the only priest in our group, but when we gathered in a huddle at Red Rock Canyon, we all took turns praying for Michael on his birthday. **There's something so powerful about a group of guys praying together for each other!** And we sat in the first row for the Blue Man Group show, and got covered with pudding and paint or whatever it is that they throw from the stage! I even got to my first Vegas latenight club! We got there after midnight and it was after 3:00 AM when we left! My head will eventually stop throbbing from the loud music there! We laughed and joked and talked and ate and drank. Most of the guys are performers and one of them (Brandon) does a skit in which he sings and dances and acts his way through the entire WIZARD OF OZ story in just about 60 seconds! At 32, he was the youngest in our group that day; at 61, I was the oldest. **And I kept up with them every step of the way!**

I have to point out that when guys go out (no matter what their ages), it is very different from when girls go out! Girls call each other by their proper names (Mary/Sue/Helen). Guys use nicknames (Dude/Sleeper/Pumpkin Butt). And when the check arrives, females tend to dissect it into who had what, and then everyone chips in the perfectly proper amount. When guys go out and the check arrives, everyone either throws $20's at it, or someone grabs it and says: **"I've got this one!"** So that was my week, and I had more fun than I even thought possible! I love my friends!

It's hard to imagine how different our lives would be without our friends. I like to think that among the many blessings that God places in our lives, one of the chief blessings is the gift of a few good and solid friendships. Oh, there are many people we talk to and maybe even hang out with, but how many are **REAL FRIENDS**? A few weeks ago, I got an email about friendship that I thought was particularly good. It was simply called **REAL FRIENDS**. I'd like to pass it on to you today:

A simple friend will stand by you when you're right, but a **REAL FRIEND** will stand by you even when you're wrong.

A simple friend opens a conversation with the full news bulletin of his/her own life. A **REAL FRIEND** says: "What's new with you?"

A simple friend has never seen you cry. A **REAL FRIEND** has a shoulder soggy with your tears.

A simple friend brings a bottle of wine to your dinner party. A **REAL FRIEND** comes early to help you cook, and stays late to help you clean up.

A simple friend thinks the problems you whine about are recent. A **REAL FRIEND** says: "Dude, you've been whining about that same thing for 14 years. Get off your duff and do something about it!"

A simple friend hates it when you call after he/she has gone to bed. A **REAL FRIEND** wonders what took you so long.

A simple friend wonders about your romantic history. A **REAL FRIEND** could blackmail you with it.

A simple friend thinks the friendship is over when you have an argument. A **REAL FRIEND** knows that it's not friendship until after you've had a fight.

A simple friend expects you to always be there for him/her. A **REAL FRIEND** expects to always be there for you.

A simple friend will bail you out of jail. A **REAL FRIEND** will be sitting beside you in the cell saying: "That was fun!"

In today's Gospel, four friends carry a paralyzed friend to Jesus. When they are unable to make it through the crowd with him, they climb up on the roof with their friend, open up the roof tiles, and lower their friend down on a mat right in front of Jesus. Now that's certainly real friendship! But even more wonderful is Jesus' response to the situation. According to the Gospel, when Jesus saw their faith (THE FAITH OF THE FOUR FRIENDS), He says to the paralyzed man: "Your sins are forgiven" and then He follows it with: "Rise, pick up your mat and walk."

The man's inner spiritual healing as well as his outer physical healing are both the result of the faith of his friends. It was their efforts and their faith in Jesus that brought about the marvelous results. We might owe a whole lot more to our friends that we usually think.

Today might be a great day to think about our real friends and at least offer a prayer of thanksgiving to God for putting them into our lives. And maybe we could resolve to be real friends to those in our own groups who depend upon us and the friendship we share with them.

God bless you!

Yes, that is a tattoo sleeve!

✤ ✤ ✤

First Sunday of Lent - "B"

1 March 2009

FIRST READING: Genesis 9:8-15
PSALM: Psalm 25:4-9
SECOND READING: 1 Peter 3:18-22
GOSPEL: Mark 1:12-15

In the Gospel today, Jesus is tempted by the devil in the desert, and He proclaims that the Kingdom of God is now at hand.

Father Michael Moore of the St. Patrick Fathers preached all the Masses on this First Sunday of Lent here at St. John the Baptist. He then gave an amazing and spiritually uplifting retreat in the four days that followed the weekend.

Second Sunday of Lent - "B"

8 March 2009

FIRST READING: Genesis 22:1-2, 9a, 10-13, 15-18
PSALM: Psalm 116:10, 15-19
SECOND READING: Romans 8:31b-34
GOSPEL: Mark 9:2-10

In the Gospel today, Jesus takes Peter, James and John up Mount Tabor and shows them a glimpse of His eternal glory.

It's the Second Sunday of Lent here in Paradise! And there's a lot going on! I'm not going to bore you with fabulous food stories. I've given that up for Lent..... not only the stories, but the food too! 30 people joined our Lenten Weigh-In, and we started with a total weight of 5512.4 pounds (That's almost two and a half tons!). Not everyone has updated their weight this week, but our gross weight is down to 5483.6 pounds - a group weight loss of 28.8 pounds! I'm walking 3 miles a day so I've already walked 33 miles this Lent! And my friend, Michael, is coaching me. He told me that I needed to convert. I told him I was Catholic and intended to stay that way! Then he smacked me and told me that I needed to convert fat into muscle. Oh...that's different! I am learning some things. Apparently coffee is a dehydrator, so I'm supposed to drink two glasses of water for every cup of coffee I drink every day. I drink a lot of coffee, so now I'm drinking a lot of water too! I feel like Lake Mead by the end of the day! **And Michael is as stubborn as I am**. He calls each night at midnight to harass me into following his instructions for exercise and nutrition.

Our Friday 6:00 AM Tiger Masses and 6:00 PM Stations of the Cross/Soup Suppers are very popular devotions this Lent. There's still some Fridays left in Lent, so feel free to come and join in them. Father Michael Moore was a thoroughly wonderful house-guest with me in the rectory, and the parish mission attracted about 150 people each of the four days this past week. Father Moore brings a tremendous spirit and real holiness which he shares so generously. He will definitely be back with us. And he's very grateful for the more than $5300.00 donated to the St. Patrick's Fathers by our parishioners.

In last week's bulletin, I shared my joy in noting that on Valentine's Day weekend, we had 2036 people at our Masses, more than on any other weekend in our history. Well, we broke that record last weekend with 2079 people joining us for Mass. So we have a new high to celebrate! I know I don't always please everyone, and I know as a group we can't always please everyone, but we sure seem to be known as a very inviting community of faith here in Laughlin. And that wouldn't happen without all of you. Keep up the great work of making people feel at home with us at Mass in the casino or in the church. We want to be the people God wants us to be.

And I have to tell you that as of Saturday morning, I am enjoying fame on YouTube all over the world! Remember a few weeks ago when I mentioned that my buddy Nick wanted me to send him some pictures of my balancing a show on my head? Well, he created a song, put together a video, and it went public on YouTube on Saturday morning. So if you want to see several pictures of your local priest balancing a show on his head, just go to You-Tube and type in the words "Shoe on Head Rap." I wonder if Bishop Pepe watches YouTube? I guess I'll find out.

Some years ago, I was privileged to make a pilgrimage to Israel with a group of people that included many priests and sisters. A few weeks before we left, we priests put our names into a lottery to see which of us would be the main celebrants for the Masses during the trip. I hoped that I would be the one chosen for the Mass at Bethlehem where Jesus was born, or maybe for the Mass at the Church of the Holy Sepulchre in Jerusalem which marks the spot of Jesus' burial. Or maybe I would get the Mass at Cana in Galilee where Jesus worked His first miracle of changing water into wine. Or maybe the Mass on Mount Tabor where Jesus was transfigured before His Apostles. Well, when the names were drawn, I did get drawn for a Mass as part of the pilgrimage. I got the Mass in the departure lounge at Kennedy Airport! Oh well, at least I could join in the other Masses along the way.

The pilgrimage was wonderful and among the best places we visited was Mount Tabor, the scene of the Transfiguration about which we read in today's Gospel from St. Mark. The view from Mount Tabor is so impressive! You can look down over the Sea of Galilee and see a vista of where Jesus did so much of His preaching and teaching. And off to another direction, you can see the Plain of Megiddo, the legendary Armageddon, where the prophets tell us the final battle between good and evil will take place at the end of the world. Even today, just to stand on Mount Tabor is memorable and thought-provoking.

Today's Gospel is the very familiar story of the Trans-figuration. Jesus takes Peter, James and John - three of His most trusted disciples - up on the mountain and there He is transfigured. His divine nature shows through His human nature. The three disciples are dumb-struck and don't know that to do.

As often as we have heard this passage, you and I may have missed its message. I have always liked the thought of seeing Christ in all His glory as God. But just think for a moment about the reaction of the disciples. Confronted with this display of God's awesomeness, they were so stunned that they didn't know what to do, so they decided to really do nothing: "Lord, it is good for us to be here, let us set up three tents.....let's just stay here." Confronted with the undeniable presence of God, the disciples just wanted to remain still in His presence. And it is only after this expression of pausing, stopping and waiting, that the voice of the Father is heard: "THIS IS MY BELOVED SON...LISTEN TO HIM!"

Perhaps if we learn to pause, to wait, to stop occasionally in the presence of God, we too might be able to hear what God has in mind for us. We pray today that this holy season of Lent will be an occasion for each of us to pause, to wait, to stop and really try to hear what God is saying to each one of us. God is waiting to transform us too. And to let His Divine Presence shine on the world through us. I repeat what I said when Lent began.....it doesn't matter one bit **WHAT** you choose to do for Lent, but it does matter a whole lot **THAT** you choose to do something during these 40 days that will bring you closer to God. There's still time. Don't waste any of the remaining days of Lent. Even taking a little time each day to be still and really listen to what God is saying to you in your heart is a beautiful way to observe Lent.

God bless you!

Third Sunday of Lent - "B"

15 March 2009

FIRST READING: Exodus 20:1-17
PSALM: Psalm 19:8-11
SECOND READING: 1 Corinthians 1:22-25
GOSPEL: John 2:13-25

Because of the RCIA program, we used the Cycle A Readings for this Sunday, and they are as follows:

FIRST READING: Exodus 17: 3-7
PSALM: Psalm 95
SECOND READING: Romans 5: 1-2. 5-8
GOSPEL: John 4: 5-42

In the Gospel today, Jesus meets the unnamed Samaritan woman at the well and discusses with her the living water He has come to bring for all His people.

What a great week in Paradise! Lent is progressing beautifully. The 30 people in our weigh-in group have collectively lost over 49 pounds since Lent began.....and we're still on the way to see who will be the biggest loser in Laughlin! I'm walking my 3 miles each day, and as of today have walked 54 miles since Lent began. Thanks to all the people who have been honking and waving as they pass by me on the roads! It sure is a lot more encouraging than the last time I tried this. I was teaching high school back in New Jersey, and my sophomores would gather as I walked/jogged around the track after school. They would yell encouraging things at me like **"Die, old man!"** People in Paradise sure are a lot nicer! I even got out to eat a few times this week, but was careful each time.....except for the one when the BBQ chicken pizza was just too much to resist! And I've been drinking more water than ever before in my life! If all our drinking water ultimately comes from Lake Mead, I'm going to be singlehandedly responsible for the lake drying up! And I learned a new game this week - FARKEL. I lost miserably, but it was fun! Who knew it could be so hard to throw dice successfully? Also went bowling up in Vegas one night at midnight. My high game was a pathetic 110, but I beat out the two younger guys I was playing against so that made me free pretty darn good. I've got such a great life here in Paradise! That's why I talk about it so much. I know I don't come close to Jesus in holiness, but I know that both Jesus and I love to talk!

In the course of His earthy ministry, Jesus did a lot of talking with people.....not only talking to them, but talking with them. And fortunately some of the Gospels give us glimpses into these conversations with Jesus. Today's Gospel gives us the conversation between Jesus and a woman at a well in Samaria. I'd suggest that this conversation is important.....not only to that Samaritan woman, but also to us. It is preserved precisely so that we could listen in on it, and learn from it. Here we see Jesus at work drawing a person away from sin and back to Himself.

First, He asked the woman for help: **"Give me a drink."** She is startled that He even spoke to her. Then He starts from the situation (she is there drawing water from a well) and begins to explain to her that her thirst for water is just a physical expression of a much greater thirst, a thirst for God. He offers the gift of living water to her.

She responds by asking Him for help: **"Give me this water."** (A reversal of the original situation.) and Jesus continues talking with her. He doesn't condemn her life (she is living with a man who is not her husband, in fact, he is the 5th person she has lived with sinfully.), but Jesus does remind her of her situation. Not unexpectedly, she immediately changes the subject. And she asks Jesus **"Where is the place where we should worship?"** And Jesus lets her go off on this tangent for awhile, but then brings her back to the situation at hand. **"The Messiah? I Who speak with you am He."** And the woman goes off and proclaims to all the townspeople that she has seen the Messiah, the Savior. And they go out to hear Jesus for themselves.

And they come back to her with words that would make any priest or religious educator thrilled beyond comparison: **"No longer does our faith depend on your story. We have heard for ourselves and we know that this really is the Savior of the world."**

So what do we learn from this Gospel? A few very important things: Jesus accepts each person exactly where he or she is, right in their own home locality, even in the midst of their sins.

Jesus then invites each person to listen to Him and to share with Him. He sometimes even asks for our help, but eventually He entices us to ask for His help in our lives.

Jesus is intent on each one of us. In the Gospel, Jesus even gave up eating with His disciples in order to spend time with this woman.

And it is good to note that Jesus did not require a Ph.D. in catechetics or a degree in Scripture Studies before He promised His gift of life to the woman. All she had to do was to respond to Him in faith.

The Samaritan woman is nameless in the Gospel. She stands for each one of us. We are accepted by Jesus right where we are, just as we are. And we are invited by Jesus to share with Him in His gift of eternal life. As this holy season of Lent progresses, we might want to think how well we respond when Jesus converses with us. Do we listen to Him? Do we enjoy our conversations (prayers) with Him? Do we make time in our lives to spend with Him? A good thought to take home today would be: **"If you're too busy to pray, then you're just too busy!"**

God bless you!

※ ※ ※

Fourth Sunday of Lent - "B"

22 March 2009

FIRST READING: 2 Chronicles 36:14-16, 19-23
PSALM: Psalm 137:1-6
SECOND READING: Ephesians 2:4-10
GOSPEL: John 3:14-21

In the Gospel today, we encounter Jesus teaching about God's plan for the world in the very famous verse John 3:16.

Yet another week has gone by here in Paradise! Friday was the first day of spring, and we had 90 degrees and sun. Back in New York/New Jersey, they had snow flurries! It just gets better and better out here! Our Lenten weigh-in group has now lost a combined weight of 80 pounds so far, and I'm betting that we pass 100 pounds by next weekend. I've walked 75 miles as of today. One night this week, I actually decided to try cooking while staying with a friend up in Vegas....so I search the fridge and decided to make an omelette. I found a frying pan, and added a pile of frozen broccoli. But it looked dull so I found a half-bag of frozen corn to add to it. Added some lemon pepper and cajun spices that I found in the kitchen. Figured I should beat up the egg first, so I put it in a large coffee mug and whipped it around with a fork. But it didn't look like it would be enough.....so I rummaged around in my friend's fridge and found some mustard to add to the egg, just a few spoonsful. But it didn't smell right so I found some light ranch dressing and added a good bit of that. Beat it all up and poured it into the frying pan and waited for it to congeal on the stove. It had kind of a weird taste, but it was supper one night. I think I'm better off going out to eat! Played a very physical game of Monopoly with two friends. Paul kept poking me and egging me on and trying to distract me. I finally reached over, grabbed him by the neck, and applied direct pressure to his carotid artery while saying: **"Ten seconds on the carotid artery and you will be quiet!"** He dared me until I really pushed down hard, and then we had an understanding for the rest of the night. My other friend Charlie won the game, but I came in second, and Paul came in third. So there will be a rematch! I emailed Paul later and accepted his challenge for whatever game he wanted to try next week.

Speaking of emails, you have to be very careful when typing an email address. One of my friends emailed me an example of what could go wrong:

A Minneapolis couple decided to come to Laughlin to thaw out during a particularly ice winter. They planned to stay at the Riverside where they had spent their honeymoon 20 years earlier. Because of their hectic schedules, it was difficult to coordinate their travel schedules. So the husband left Minnesota and flew to Laughlin on Thursday, with his wife scheduled to come down on the following day. The husband checked into the hotel. There was a computer in his room, so he decided to send an email to his wife. HOWEVER, he accidentally left out one letter in her email address, and without realizing his error, he sent the email.

Meanwhile, somewhere in Houston, a widow had just returned home from her husband's funeral. He was a minister who was called home to glory following a sudden heart attack. The widow decided to check her email, expecting to find some more messages from relatives and friends. After reading the first message, she screamed and fainted. The widow's son rushed into the room, found his mother passed out on the floor, and saw the computer screen which read:

TO: My Loving Wife
FROM: Me
SUBJECT: I've arrived

I know you're surprised to hear from me. They have computers here now and you are allowed to send emails to your loved ones. I've just arrived and have been checked in. I see that everything has been prepared for your arrival tomorrow. Looking forward to seeing you then! Hope your journey will be as uneventful as mine.

P.S......Sure is freaking hot down here!

So, be careful the next time you send an email to someone you love! I love comedy and I love hearing jokes and telling them. And thanks to email, I have a never-ending supply coming to me each week. I'm convinced that many of my friends really don't work at the office. They just spend their days emailing me!

The only problem with jokes is that it is so hard to remember them so you can tell them correctly. You need a good memory for that. Actually, I think that memory serves a much more important purpose as we get older. It keeps alive people and events that have become important in our lives..... and the older we get, the more people and events we have to remember. And certainly God gave us our memories so that we could remember Him and all that He has done for us. Each Sunday at Mass, each time we read the Bible, each time we pray, we are strengthening and sharpening our memories, remembering more and more vividly all that God has done for us. We remember so that we can appreciate all over again how good God is and how much we need Him.

God wanted the Israelites to remember His saving acts throughout their long history.....and they wrote the Bible so that they would never forget all that God had done for them. The Bible is really the history book of salvation. Right now, in this holy season of Lent, you and I are in the process of writing our own personal histories of salvation. This week, resolve at least once to think about God's powerful word to us in John 3:16 from today's Gospel. It really is the Bible's whole message in one single verse:

What is God's relationship with us?
GOD LOVES US.
What does God do for us?
GOD SENDS JESUS, HIS OWN SON, TO SAVE US.
What do we have to do?
BELIEVE IN JESUS AND HIS SAVING WORKS.
What do we get out of all this?
WE GET ETERNAL LIFE WITH GOD IN HEAVEN.

Here is a piece of God's word that is well worth committing to our memories: John 3:16 - **"For God so loved the world that He gave His only Son, so that everyone who believes in Him might not perish, but might have eternal life."**

Let's try to remember it always!

God bless you!

Fifth Sunday of Lent - "B"

29 March 2009

FIRST READING: Jeremiah 31:31-34
PSALM: Psalm 51:3-4, 12-15
SECOND READING: Hebrews 5:7-9
GOSPEL: John 12:20-33

In the Gospel today, Jesus teaches that He will be put to death, but because of His death, He will bring the fruit of salvation to all the world.

Another awesome week in Paradise! Collectively, our parish Lenten weigh-in group has lost 96 pounds since Lent began. Everyone needs to weigh in before Easter so we can tally the final results. Father Peter and I had lunch on Monday. Since we ate on his side of the river, he paid and I got treated. Can't complain about that! On my own Lenten diet, I've managed to lose 17 pounds and have walked 96 miles since Lent began. One of our parishioners was telling me about a new diet - the MERLOT and RAW CABBAGE diet. You can drink all the MERLOT and eat all the RAW CABBAGE you want. Eventually you stop eating the cabbage and just don't care about how much you weigh! Got to see my young friend Eddie starring in the Las Vegas production of "Thoroughly Modern Millie." Awesome show, and I felt like a proud parent sitting in the front row watching him on stage. And yesterday, a long-time penpal from Australia was passing through town, so we got to actually meet each other. And Australians really do say things like "G'Day, mate!" We had a lot of fun actually hearing each other's voice. Friends are an awesome part of life in Laughlin, and wherever we are.

Whenever some mother or father complains to me that they just don't understand the behavior of their sons or daughters, or the friends they hang around with, I always think back to my own youth.

In my teens, my friend Mike and I ganged up on his little brother, Jimmy, and one Christmas Eve, we sealed him in a cardboard box. He's never forgotten it! Even as recently as last year when Mike and Jimmy and I were having dinner with their wives and children, as soon as Jimmy said something we didn't agree with, Mike and I would stand up, look right at Jimmy, and say: **"Get the box!"** And he would start to twitch! Ah, we warped that kid's mind for sure!

In my 20's, my friend Tommy and I once devised a way to stop his little brother, Billy, from bothering us. It was the 1970's. We all worked together at any office. Billy had the long blond hair so popular back then. So we took Billy into the bathroom one day, turned him upside down, dipped his head in the toilet bowl, and mopped the bathroom floor with his blond hair!

One Christmas Eve, John and a few of my other friends ganged up on me in the seminary. They tied me up in a burlap sack, dragged me down four flights of stone steps, and were attempting to throw me into the back seat of a car to leave me in some desolate spot.....just for fun!.....when someone intervened and stopped them.

My friend, Len, ended up in the hospital with appendicitis. I wanted to cheer him up so I used my Roman collar to get into the hospital after normal visiting hours one night and I took pictures of him in his hospital bed. The flashes brought the nurses running! And I posted the pictures on the school bulletin board where he was teaching.

In high school, my friend, Paul, and I were thrown out of the United Nations building in New York City, and escorted by the security guards to the sidewalk after we tried to use fake ID's to get into a secure delegate area. A bit embarrassing.....but still a lot of fun!

The amazing thing is that even today when these old friends and I get together, we still tell the old stories and we still look at the old pictures and we still look for fun things to do together. And I think our families still worry a lot about us!

Old friends are the best! We not only have fun in the present time, but we draw upon our memories of a shared past. Something like that same dynamic is true in religion as well. We have a shared past with those who have gone before us in the Faith, and we can draw upon that shared past in the present time. That's one of the reasons, by the way, why the reading of the Scriptures at Mass is always so important...it reminds us of our "old friends", our shared past with those who have gone before us. The Prophet Jeremiah tells us that not only was God so close to our spiritual ancestors that He took them by their hands to lead them, but that they and we can be so close to Him that God will write His law upon our hearts. Just imagine how close that makes God to us! His law is written within us. And the Letter to the Hebrews reminds us that Jesus is our source of eternal salvation. And St. John's Gospel talks about us becoming more like Christ Himself by learning to serve Him and to follow His example in our lives even when it involves suffering. Jesus has the glory of God Himself and He wants to share that glory with us as we become more like Him in this life. We need to be close to Him.

Each Sunday at Mass, we gather with some of our old friends in the Scriptures and we relearn what it is like to be close to them. And we also gather with our newer friends - this congregation - so we can strengthen one another through our prayers and our good examples. We draw strength from one another. That's just one of the many reasons why it is so vitally important to gather here each week so we can learn and strengthen and increase our Faith. The Lord even promises to be with us when we gather here. He's present in the Scriptures and He's physically present in the Eucharist. Old friends are the best, and the Lord Himself is our oldest Friend! He's been with us throughout our lives. He knows all about us, and He can do wonders with us and within us. As Lent progresses, we need to spend some time with Him and enjoy the best of Friends we could possibly have.

God bless you!

Palm Sunday of the Lord's Passion - "B"

5 April 2009

FIRST READING: Isaiah 50:4-7
PSALM: Psalm 22:8-9, 17-18a, 19-20, 23-24
SECOND READING: Philippians 2:6-11
GOSPEL: Mark 14:1-15:47

In the Gospel today, Jesus suffers and dies for the salvation of the world.

On Palm Sunday, the reading of the Passion of Jesus Christ does not need a sermon to elaborate on the very words of the Scriptures. There is no sermon on Palm Sunday because there is nothing I could say that would in any way make the words and actions of Jesus in His final hours any more powerful than they are in the Gospel themselves.

Easter Sunday - "B"

12 April 2009

FIRST READING: Acts 10:34a, 37-43
PSALM: Psalm 118:1-2, 16a-17, 22-23
SECOND READING: Colossians 3:1-4
GOSPEL: Mark 16:1-7

In the Gospel today, Mary Magdalene and some other faithful women find Jesus' empty tomb. He is not there, He has risen from the dead!

Welcome to Easter in Paradise! For those of you from St. John the Baptist here in Laughlin, you already know how happy I am to be here! It's my 35th Easter as a priest, and my 1st Easter with you as your administrator. There is no place else on earth that I would rather be! And I'm thrilled that you're all here to celebrate Easter with me! Parishioners and visitors alike.....you are all part of my dream come true to be here in Nevada! It's going to be in the 80's and sunny here today.....New Jersey was never like this on Easter!

So far, I can document that our Lenten weigh-in group collectively lost 123.4 pounds. 28.2 of those pounds were mine! So that's something else to celebrate! For all the years that my Mom was alive, she would always buy me a stuffed rabbit for Easter, and I've continued that tradition since she died. So every year, I will have a new rabbit to show you.

I have a very simple story for you this Easter. The teacher gave his 5th grade class an assignment. Go home and get their parents to tell them a story with a moral at the end of it. The next day, the kids came back and one by one began to tell their stories.

Ashley said, "My father is a farmer and we have a lot of egg-laying hens. One time we were taking our eggs to the market in a basket on the front seat of the car. We hit a big bump in the road and all the eggs went flying, and broke, and made a big mess." "So what's the moral of your story?" asked the teacher. And Ashley replied, "Don't put all your eggs in one basket." "Very good," said the teacher.

Next, little Sarah raised her hand, and said, "Our family are farmers too. But we raise chickens for the meat market. One time we had a dozen eggs, but when they hatched, we only got ten live chickens. The moral of this story is *Don't count your chickens before they hatch*." "That was a fine story, Sarah," said the teacher.

Then the teacher said, "Michael, do you have a story with a moral to tell us from your family?" And Michael replied, "Yes, my daddy told me this story about my Aunt Karen. Aunt Karen was a flight engineer in the First Gulf War. Her plane got hit and she had to bail out over enemy territory. And besides her parachute, all she had was a full bottle of whiskey, a gun, and a knife. She drank the whiskey on the way down so it wouldn't break. She landed right in the middle of 100 enemy troops. With the gun, she got rid of 80 of them before she ran out of bullets. Then, with the knife, she got rid of 15 of them until the knife blade broke. Then she beat up the last 5 with her bare hands." "Good heavens," said the horrified teacher, "What possible moral did your daddy teach you from that horrible story?" And Michael said, "Stay away from Aunt Karen when she's been drinking!"

So what's the moral of the Easter story....the horrible suffering and death of Jesus on Good Friday, and His glorious resurrection on Easter Sunday?

Easter is the pre-eminent celebration of hope and new life. It's a celebration of all the wild possibilities for goodness and happiness that the future holds in store for each and every one of us. It's a yearly reminder of the grace and love with which our God cares for us from our birth until we join Him in eternity. Even death cannot limits God's love and grace and care for us.

It's interesting (and even a bit ironic!) how many people come to church on Easter who let other things take the place of God in their lives for the rest of the year. It's probably a good thing, though, that at least at Easter they attempt to fulfill God's command to be present to worship Him. But when you think about it, NO ONE BUT JESUS WAS PRESENT when the Resurrection actually happened. The women and the disciples only came along later, and they became witnesses to the empty tomb.

But it is vitally important that we gather for Easter, that along with Christians throughout the world and down through the ages, we celebrate together that Christ is risen. Easter reminds us each year that death is not the end, that there is a whole lot more to life than what we can see and appreciate during our relatively few years here on earth. If it were not for the Resurrection of Jesus, you and I might be tempted to just give up when things get rough or when loved ones get sick or die. We might mistakenly think that life is only what we can see or touch. We might fail to realize that life, real life, is a whole lot more.

People knew that Jesus had risen from the dead because they saw the results of the Resurrection in the lives of Jesus' followers. It was their lives that made the Resurrection so convincing. This Easter, I would like to suggest to all of you that it is truly OUR LIVES which continue to make the Resurrection so convincing. If we do not live as people who believe in the Resurrection, then there really is no other way for people to see it's truth in our world today. We are very important to God in spreading His message of hope throughout the world.

Sure there will sometimes be obstacles, but we have the strength and power of God behind us when we choose to do what is right, even when it is difficult or even unpopular. And that's the awesome moral of the Easter story.....God has given us all hope of second chances and eternal life.

May we always live our lives as people who truly believe that Jesus Christ is the Lord of our lives, the One Who has conquered sin and death for all eternity.

Happy Easter from all of us here at St. John the Baptist in scenic Laughlin along the banks for the Colorado River to all of you from near or far.

God bless you!

❖ ❖ ❖

Second Sunday of Easter - "B"

19 April 2009

FIRST READING: Acts 4:32-35
PSALM: Psalm 118:2-4, 13-15, 22-24
SECOND READING: 1 John 5:1-6
GOSPEL: John 20:19-31

In the Gospel today, Jesus shares His peace and His limitless mercy with His Disciples.

Easter in Paradise! What an incredibly beautiful Easter we had last weekend! Nearly 1900 people joined us for the Easter Masses. Our Easter collection so far has exceeded $12,000.00, not counting the several thousand dollars donated to our building fund. Four candidates completed their sacraments of initiation at the Easter Vigil and I got to administer the Sacrament of Confirmation to them (that's the closest I'll ever get to being a bishop!) I had a wonderful lobster tail dinner on Easter Sunday night (where else but in Laughlin can you get TWO lobster tails with vegetables and rice for only $19.95!) I love this place! I took a walk along the river on Easter Sunday afternoon and all I could think of was that we are so blessed to be living here or visiting here. We have so much to be thankful for!

There are many names for the Sunday after Easter. At various times and in various places, it has been called LOW SUNDAY (because of the drop in attendance compared with Easter); SUNDAY IN WHITE (because the newly-baptized used to wear their white garments to Mass for the Sunday following Easter); DIVINE MERCY SUNDAY (in honor of the celebration of Jesus' unlimited mercy to all of us). But my personal favorite has always been a medieval tradition of calling this Sunday after Easter BRIGHT SUNDAY, a day on which we renew our Easter joy. We, as faithful Catholic Christians, can laugh in triumph over the devil. In the big picture, he's just a COSMIC LOSER in the battle for our souls! We can LAUGH at him because JESUS is the ULTIMATE WINNER. And you and I are associated with Jesus' victory over sin and death because of our baptism.

During a speech to priests about preaching, Bishop Robert Morneau of Green Bay, Wisconsin, said: **"If you can make your people smile even a little bit on a Sunday when they come to Mass, do it. They've had a hard week and it is good for them to laugh in church."** I try to follow that advice whenever possible.

Many of us who come to church faithfully no doubt bring worries and cares with us. And we can't just check them at the door, or turn them off like we do our cell phones before entering here. Certainly we are concerned with the Middle East, and the safety of our American Forces overseas, particularly in Iraq and Afghanistan. Certainly we're concerned with terrorist activities. Certainly we're concerned with situations within our own families of divorce, death or sickness of a spouse or parent or child, bread-winners being out of work, and so many other situations in life. We have to hold on to the belief that God is still in charge. And while we might feel there is very little we can do as individuals in these various crises, we can most certainly pray that God will shed His light and give to us and to those in authority the wisdom they need to deal with these situations. And we can also pray that those whose lives have been affected might find the peace and healing that only Jesus can provide. These situations may certainly TEST our Faith, but they should never be allowed to weaken it or destroy it. Like Thomas in today's Gospel, we need the re-assurance of Jesus. And Jesus re-assures us too. He invites our belief. He does not force us to believe. And even when we fail, God's mercy is boundless and undeservedly generous. You'll see in the bulletin that today we celebrate Divine Mercy Sunday, so a few brief stories about mercy are appropriate. Let me tell you about a Photographer's Mercy, Desert Mercy, New York Mercy, and God's Mercy.

PHOTOGRAPHER'S MERCY: The story is told of a politician who looked at the proofs of his pictures and was very angry with the photographer. He stormed into the man's office and screamed at him: "These pictures do not do me justice!" And the photographer calmly replied: "Sir, with a face like yours, what you need is mercy, not justice!"

DESERT MERCY: Three men lose their way in the desert and are captured by a wandering desert tribe. The Sultan sentences them to death, but says he would spare them on one condition. Each man had to go to the local food store and select five pieces of the same kind of fruit. The first man to return had five large tomatoes. He was told that he must swallow all five whole without making any kind of facial expression or sound. As he swallowed the last and largest tomato, he screamed in pain...and so he was executed. The second man brought back five blueberries. He swallowed the first four with no problem, but as he was swallowing the fifth blueberry, he burst out laughing. Before he was executed, the Sultan asked him to explain why he had laughed. He pointed to the third man who was just coming back from the store with five large pineapples!

NEW YORK MERCY: Now we're getting into a true story. One night in 1935, Mayor Fiorello LaGuardia of New York City showed up at a night court in the poorest ward in the city. He dismissed the judge for the evening and took over the bench. One cases involved an elderly grandmother who was caught stealing bread to feed her grandchildren. LaGuardia said, "I've got to punish you, the law is the law. I sentence you to a fine of $10 or ten days in jail." As he spoke, he threw a $10 bill into his hat. He then fined everyone in the courtroom 50 cents for living in a city "where an old woman had to stead bread so that her grandchildren should not starve." He passed the hat around, and the woman left the courtroom with her fine paid, and an additional $47.50 in her pocket.

And finally.....GOD'S MERCY: A man dies and goes to heaven. Of course, St. Peter meets him at the Pearly Gates. St. Peter says, "Here's how it works. You need 100 points to make it into heaven. You tell me all the good things you've done, and I will give you a certain number of points for each item, depending on how good it was. When you reach 100 points, you get in to heaven." "Okay," the man says, "I was married to the same woman for 50 years and never once cheated on her, even in my heart." "That's wonderful," says St. Peter, "that's worth three points!" "Three points!?!?" says the man. "Well, I attended church all my life and supported the ministry with my tithes and service." "Terrific!" says St. Peter. "That's certainly worth a point." "One point!?!?" screams the man. "I started a soup kitchen in my city and I worked in a shelter for homeless veterans." "Fantastic, that's good for two more points," says St. Peter. Exasperated, the man screams, "Two points!?!?.....At this rate, the only way I'll get into heaven is by the grace and mercy of God!" "Bingo," says St. Peter, "Now you understand! Come on in!"

We all need God's mercy. Think of how merciful God has been to you.....and then try to imitate God's mercy with each other.

God bless you!

Third Sunday of Easter - "B"

26 April 2009

FIRST READING: Acts 3:13-15, 17-19
PSALM: Psalm 4:2, 4, 7-9
SECOND READING: 1 John 2:1-5a
GOSPEL: Luke 24:35-48

In the Gospel today, Jesus reassures His followers that He remains with them, that He is alive, and that He is real.

What an awesome week in Paradise! A box of Cinnabons got dropped off at the office, but I sort of stuck to my diet and only ate one of them! I've never been in Laughlin for River Run, so I didn't quite know what to expect. When I mentioned to some parishioners that I was going down to Casino Drive, one man told me, **"You can't do that...you'll have to send your eyes to confession!"** But I went down anyway.....several times.....and I loved it! There's some awesome music and incredible bikes and more tattoos than I've ever seen in one place in my life! I even stopped by the tattoo convention and watched the process being done...but resisted the urge to get one myself. I met a few parishioners who would stare at me as I walked by, then kind of blink their eyes, and finally say, "Father?" I did buy some Harley socks to wear and got a great Biker Week shirt as a gift. One of the two best parts of the week for me was when one of our parishioners, Jeff, invited me to ride with him on his Honda

Goldwings Trike! I'd never been on one before! It was AWESOME! We rode from the church down to Casino Drive, then over the bridge, down Route 95, past the AVI, and then back to the church. I've got to do that again! I think one of our parishioners spotted me riding on the Trike.....as we drove past the Edgewater, I saw this man just pointing his arm with his mouth wide open as we went by! The other best part of the week for me was discovering that the American Madmen were in town doing a show each night at the Pioneer! They're two guys (Ses Carny and Wyck) who do a seriously dangerous carnival sideshow involving throwing knives at each other, catching an arm in a beartrap, hanging hooks from Ses' eyes, breathing fire, and hammering a nail up one of their noses. I'm a huge sideshow fan, so this was incredible for me! And since I was standing right up against the stage, I got to join in the audience participation part at the end of the show. For a buck, you could staple the money to their arms, chest or back with a staple gun! In fact, I had so much fun at the show on Thursday night, that I went back again on Friday night! Laughlin just keeps getting better and better for me! Some days it's hard for me to believe that I'm really here and all this good stuff is really happening to me!

I'm sure that same thought crossed the minds of Jesus' Apostles many times when Jesus appeared to them after His Resurrection from the dead.... could this really be happening?

Perhaps that's one of the reasons why they had such difficulty in believing that Jesus was really alive and had come back from the dead. Perhaps some of these questions and emotions still cloud our minds today and keep us from fully believing in God's presence in our lives and in the life of the world.

There is a true story about a judge in Yugoslavia who had an unfortunate accident. He was electrocuted when he reached up to turn on the light while standing in the bathtub. His wife found his body sprawled on the bathroom floor. She called for help - friends, neighbors, police - everyone showed up. He was pronounced dead and taken to the funeral home. The local radio station picked up the story and broadcast it all over the area. In the middle of the night, the judge regained consciousness. When he realized where he was, he rushed over to alert the night watchman, who promptly ran off, terrified. The first thought of the judge was to phone his wife and reassure her. But he got no further than "Hello, darling, it's me," when she screamed and then fainted. He tried calling a couple of the neighbors but they all thought that it was some sort of sick prank. He even went so far as to go the homes of several friends, but they were all sure he was a ghost and they slammed their doors in his face. Finally he was able to call a friend in the next town who hadn't heard about his death. This friend was able to come and convince his family and other friends that he really was alive.

Jesus had to convince His disciples that He wasn't a ghost. He had to dispel their doubts and their fears. He showed them His hands and His feet. He invited them to touch Him and to seed that He was real. He even ate a piece of cooked fish with them - all to prove that He was alive and not a ghost or a spirit. He stood there before them as real and as alive as He had been before His death.

And over and over again, Jesus reassured them with the greeting "Peace be with you."

Just imagine the incredible patience of God as He tries to convince these human beings of the awesome miracle that has occurred! Just imagine how patient God is with us when we're just as slow and as dull to believe as the Apostles and disciples were. What will it take to make us believe that Jesus really rose from the dead? That Jesus really is alive? That Jesus really did establish a Church and tell us how to live?

If I were God, I would have given up on us a long time ago! But God has not given up on us! Even when we're dull and slow to believe, even when we fail to live up to the teachings of our Catholic Faith, even when we let all sorts of lesser things influence us more than our beliefs, even when we don't teach our families the importance of faithfulness, even when we run out of Mass needlessly early so as not to spend even an extra minute with God, even then.....God still tries to convince us that He's real and that He wants us to be close to Him.

What will it take for us to believe? God is patient, and He'll keep in trying. He never gives up on us. And for that, we should thank God!

God bless you!

A little fun with an Evil Clown at River Run!

Fourth Sunday of Easter - "B"

3 May 2009

FIRST READING: Acts 4:8-12
PSALM: Psalm 118:1, 8-9, 21-23, 26, 28-29
SECOND READING: 1 John 3:1-2
GOSPEL: John 10:11-18

In the Gospel today, Jesus names Himself the "Good Shepherd", the One who leads and protects His flock.

Other than missing the bikers, it was another great week in Paradise! I had so much fun during River Run that I'm already looking forward to it next year! Been watching American Idol with some friends who are professional singers. It's amazing how differently we see things on the show! The ones I like, they don't. Had some amazing garlic/onion mashed potatoes given to me this week, as well as some truly incredible homemade New England clam chowder served in warm semolina bread bowls. That had to hurt the diet! Was up in Vegas to hang out with some friends and to meet their most recent girlfriends. My policy is: don't tell me their names unless you plan on staying together for a long time. I only have a limited amount of brain cells and I don't want to waste them on changing information! Celebrated the ground-breaking for the new Colorado River Food Bank building here in Laughlin. They do so much good for our community! And attended the Vicariate meeting for priests in the Southern Region of the Diocese of Las Vegas. I got introduced as "This is Charlie from Laughlin where he's always smiling!" Some of the priests, I think, are getting curious about how awesome it is down here....so I'm going to have to start holding back on telling them what a great community we have! Otherwise, they'll start wanting to come here!

Today at the 8:00 AM Mass, we celebrated First Holy Communion with six of our parish children. Hope Castillo has done a wonderful job of preparing them for this milestone in their religious development. From my own point of view, I was thrilled to see another group come forward to receive Jesus for the first time.

Of course, I thought back to my own First Holy Communion in May of 1955 - 54 years ago! I received my First Holy Communion before the parents of our present First Holy Communicants were even born! For my First Holy Communion, I was dressed in a pure white suit and tie. I looked like a cheap imitation of John Travolta in "Saturday Night Fever!" I remember going out to the Lyndhurst Diner with my parents and spilling an entire glass of fresh orange juice down the front of the suit. Could never get that stain out!

I'm sure if you think about it, you can recall your own First Holy Communion day. It had to feel special to receive Jesus for the very first time in your life whether it was in a big cathedral or even in a small country church!

Along with a letter from me congratulating them, I also include a little sign to post on the refrigerator at home. As you can see, I am not subtle about it at all! Catholics go to Mass every Sunday. It's just what we do! And I know parents like to have my helpful reminder.

While I'm on the topic of Communion, it might be good to offer a reminder to those who do come faithfully to Mass about how to receive Communion. We make a slight bow of our heads as we approach for Communion. Then, if you are receiving the host on your tongue, you need to come forward and actually open your mouth with your tongue out! I'm not going to reach in there! If you're going to receive Communion in your hand, then you need to hold your hands out, one over the other, and form a flat surface for me to place the Host on. It's not a bowl, not crossed fingers, and not grabbing the Host out of my hand! As one ancient saint put it, you are forming a throne on which the King of the Universe will be placed. And, of course, things like gum and candy should not be in your mouth in church anyway.

And given the current swine flu from Mexico, it is good to be reminded that we should be careful to wash out hands frequently. And if the person sitting next to you would prefer not to shake hands at the Sign of Peace, that's okay. And, of course, no one should receive the Precious Blood of Christ from the chalice if they have any flu-like symptoms. In receiving the Consecrated Host, you are already receiving the BODY, BLOOD, SOUL AND DIVINITY OF CHRIST.

Today is Good Shepherd Sunday, and Jesus tells us in the Gospel that He is the Good Shepherd Who watches over us and guides us. So today, as we come up for Communion, whether it is our second or our 12,000th, breathe a prayer of gratitude to God for loving us so much. And pray for your own parents and those teachers who have helped you to remain faithful along the way.

We have something that no one else in the world has access to in the same way. Those who are not Catholic, or those Catholics not living their Catholic Faith as they should are not allowed to received Jesus in Communion. In time, that's usually what leads people to come back to regular worship, or to get their marriages validated and blessed in the Catholic Church, or to go to confession to have their sins forgiven. They miss Communion so much. Communion is a great gift and privilege for those who are trying to be faithful. God loves us so much that He actually chooses to come to us in this special way. If you think about that, it is really mind-boggling! And it should make every Sunday a special day in our lives as we come together to receive the Lord Jesus Christ.

First Holy Communion Day is a real blessing for those receiving Jesus for the very first time, and for our whole community. It reminds us just how blessed we are to have God so close to us.

God bless you!

Fifth Sunday of Easter - "B"

10 May 2009

FIRST READING: Acts 9:26-31
PSALM: Psalm 22:26-27, 28, 30-32
SECOND READING: 1 John 3:18-24
GOSPEL: John 15: 1-8

In the Gospel today, Jesus teaches about the importance of being connected with Him, just like a vine and branches are connected to each other.

What a great week this has been in Paradise! Last Saturday after Mass, I went to the Riverview Cafe for my dinner. Had a great cobb salad. When I asked for my check, the waiter pointed to a couple by the window. I didn't know them, but I went up to thank them for my dinner. Turns out they were vacationing in Laughlin from Kansas, and had just come to our 4:00 PM Mass at the Riverside. They enjoyed it so much that when they saw me come in to eat, they asked the waiter to give them my check! So now I'm even being fed by strangers! **This place is awesome!** And the Knights of Columbus took me out to dinner on last Sunday for a great Chinese buffet. And then on Wednesday, I was up in Vegas to see Tony and Tina's Wedding....great fun show and a great meal was included with it. A few years ago, I had thought about auditioning for the part of the priest in that show. Just wanted to see if I could be convincing enough as a priest to get the part!

Got two awesome gifts this week - a custard pie covered with fresh raspberries and blueberries, and a 2' x 3' poster of the American Madmen (remember the sideshow from River Run a few weeks ago!) The Pioneer gave it to me! I think I've got the only rectory in the world with a huge poster of two sideshow freaks wrapped in barbed wire hanging on my wall! And last night, I got invited out to the Beach Boys concert along the river. I even got to hear a great joke about my former homestate (New Jersey) which I know I will use with my friends back there....**Why are New Yorkers afraid to die? Because they know that the light at the end of the tunnel is New Jersey!** Golly, it's fun to live in Laughlin!

Few days in the calendar stirs the emotions that Mother's Day stirs in the hearts of all generations from little children to elderly adults. No holiday other than Christmas sees more cards sold. No other holiday sees as many families eating out in restaurants. No other holiday besides Christmas and Easter brings people out to church in such great numbers. Today we pray that God will bless our mothers, grandmothers, great-grandmothers, step-mothers, Godmothers, and all who have been like mothers to us as only He knows how. If they are still living, may He give them health and the fulfillment of all their dreams. If they have already died, may He reward their goodness with happiness in eternity.

I love Mother's Day because it stirs up so many awesome memories. For the past several weeks, I've been searching my memory for MOMisms, the collective wisdom of Moms throughout the world. I'd like to share some of them with you today:

"Be sure to wear clean underwear in case you get into an accident!" (Why, is there a place on the police report for that?)

"If you make that face again, your face will freeze into that shape!" (Yeah, right, what's the chance of that happening?)

"You'd better put a coat on, it's cold outside today." (But, Mom, it's 105 degrees in the shade and we're in Laughlin!)

"If I've told you once, I've told you a thousand times!" (Did you really count?)

"What if everyone jumped off a cliff? Would you do it too?"

"Close that door! Were you raised in a barn?"

"If you can't say something nice, don't say anything at all."

"Don't put that in your mouth! You don't know where it's been!" (I'm told that dad's have a 10 second rule....if they pick it up off the floor within 10 seconds, it doesn't matter, they just put it back into the child's mouth!)

"Just who do you think you are?!"

"Do you think your socks are going to pick themselves up?"

"What do you mean you aren't going to eat everything on your plate? Think of all those poor starving children in Asia!" (Mom, if you'll send it to them, I'll pack it up!)

"Eat those carrots, they're good for your eyesight! You never see rabbits wearing glasses, do you?"

"Don't pick on that, it'll get infected!"

"Look it up in your contract! I'm the Mom, you're the kid, I get to do the nagging!"

"If you'd open your eyes as wide as your mouth, you'd find what you're looking for!"
"So it's raining, you're not sugar, you won't melt!"

"If you swallow a watermelon seed, a watermelon will grow in your stomach!"

"Why, because I said so, that's why!"

I'm sure everyone has his/her own favorite MOMisms! And they're really universal.

One thing about mothers is that they are usually the ones who take care of the details. Everyone else makes the big plans, but Mom worries about the details of carrying out the plans. Who's going to bring the food? Did everything get packed for the trip? Who's going to take care of the dog? In honor of Mom taking care of the details, I thought I would point out two very important details in today's readings.

St. John in today's Second Reading reminds us that we are all God's children. That's something that we can easily forget as our days of school and work and life in general just get busy. But it's a vitally important detail! If we are all God's children, then we have incredible value! We are really important.... and so are all the rest of God's children. Just simply remembering this truth of our Catholic Faith should make a mighty difference in our dealings with one another. The way we treat one another is the way we treat other members of God's own family.

In today's Gospel, Jesus speaks of the vine and the branches. And He reminds us that we need to be connected with Him throughout our lives. In many ways, it was our mothers who first taught us about family and connectedness with friends and neighbors and even with God. In many ways, if we are faithful today, it is because of the lessons we learned from our mothers and those who are like mothers to us. And sometimes it is through their tireless prayers that we have come back to the Church and home when we have strayed. Never underestimate the power of a mother's prayers! As we think of our mothers today, as we honor them on this Mother's Day, we should most certainly pray for them. And we should be confident that our prayers have tremendous power. In many cases, if we think back, it was probably our mothers who first taught us to pray, and who brought us to church, and who reminded us over and over again that God loves us. What we owe to them is a debt that we can never repay. So to all our mothers, grandmothers, great-grandmothers, step-mothers, Godmothers and all those who have been like mothers to us - Have a great day! And know that your children love you!

God bless you!

Sixth Sunday of Easter - "B"

17 May 2009

FIRST READING: Acts 10:25-26, 34-35, 44-48
PSALM: Psalm 98:1-4
SECOND READING: 1 John 4:7-10
GOSPEL: John 15:9-17

In the Gospel today, Jesus shares His great commandment of love and commands His Disciples: "Love one another."

Well, we hit 110 degrees this week here in Paradise! It's going to be a really good hot summer! And it's really hard to stick with my diet when homemade sticky buns, and home-made chocolate fudge, and homemade red velvet cake have been arriving! Not to mention the grilled salmon, spinach and ricotta cheese stuffed pasta, chicken and dumplings and the brussels sprouts drizzled with olive oil and garlic. I'm going to have to walk to Vegas and back next week to work it all off!

Speaking of Las Vegas, our Bishop Joseph Pepe was with us on Sunday afternoon for Confirmation and he was a delight! As he was about to lay his hands on the head of each of those to be confirmed, he invited me to join him in doing it too. I told him that I'd never done that before, and he said: **"I know it's not in the ritual, but it looks really good!"** So he explained to the candidates that they were going to get a double-dose of the Holy Spirit because we were both going to lay hands on their heads and give them a **"Joey/ Charlie blessing!"** I don't think the bishop back in New Jersey ever even knew my first name!

Just before the Saturday night Mass last weekend, I was at the Riverside and was talking about going to see the Beach Boys that night. Two boys were hanging around and said: "Our parents are going to see the Beach Boys too!" I asked if the two boys were going, and they said: "No." And the younger one (about 7 years old) added, "I don't want to see them anyway!" I asked where they were from, and the boys said they were from California. So I said: "Well, then you should like the Beach Boys!" And the younger one said: "Why?" So his older brother said: "Because California has a beach, and we're boys!" And that settled it.

Speaking of "settling it", you'll notice in our bulletin that in the Diocese of Las Vegas, the celebration of the Ascension of the Lord is MOVED to next Sunday, so THURSDAY of this week is NOT a holyday of obligation on either side of the river. In fact, Thursday is only observed as a holyday of obligation in the provinces of New York, Hartford, New Jersey, Philadelphia, and the state of Nebraska. So we have no Masses here on Thursday because we're celebrating the Ascension of the Lord on next Sunday. St. Margaret Mary across the river is also observing the Ascension on next Sunday.

Some people have commented that my sermons the past couple of weeks have been longer than usual, so I'm just going to tell you three little stories today, and then wrap up the sermon. All I ask is that you think about the stories and see what they might suggest to you. It's sort of a do-it-yourself sermon. I figure that everyone should like at least one of the stories.

There's a beautiful story about St. John the Evangelist nearing the end of his life and being exiled to the Island of Patmos. It was there that he wrote his Gospel and his Letters. But the story says that near the end of his life, St. John used to walk around the island and stop anyone who would listen and just keep repeating over and over again: "Love one another." In the story, that became his legacy. In the Gospel, St. John is identified as "the one Jesus loved." If St. John were asked: "What is your primary identity in life?", he would probably not reply: "I am a disciple, an apostles, an evangelist, an author of one of the four Gospels." Rather he would say: "I am the one Jesus loves." Today's Gospel and Second Reading from St. John's Letters remind us that our primary identity in life as Catholic Christians should be the same. Who am I? Who are you? You and I are the ones Jesus loves. Think about that.

A priest was visiting a rural parish and was walking along a country road. He sees an old farm worker kneeling by the side of the road praying. The priest was impressed by this display of faith, and goes up to the man and says: **"You must be very close to God."** And the man looks up from his prayers, thinks for a moment, and then smiles and replies: **"Yes, He's very fond of me."** Think about that.

There's another story about a priest who arrives in his new parish and preaches a beautiful sermon on the topic of today's readings - love one another. The people are thrilled, and they are so proud of their new priest who gave such an inspiring sermon that they go out and tell everyone about it. The next Sunday the church has dozens of new faces waiting expectantly for the sermon. And the priest gives exactly, word-for-word, the same sermon as the week before. Well, the people are still impressed, but not as enthusiastic. So the next Sunday, they are waiting to hear what he has to say. And again, he gives exactly the same sermon about loving one another. So this time, some of the parishioners take him aside after the Mass and say: "Father, you gave a wonderful sermon about loving one another on your first Sunday here, but now you have repeated exactly the same sermon for several weeks. Why do you do that?" And the priest replied: **"When you start doing what I asked the first week, then we can move on."**

God is love. God loves us. If we want to be like God, we need to do the same. That's the theology, that's the reality, now you and I need to flesh it out. Let's give it our best shot here in Paradise along the beautiful Colorado River. God bless you!

❖ ❖ ❖

The Ascension of the Lord - "B"

24 May 2009

FIRST READING: Acts 1:1-11
PSALM: Psalm 47:2-3, 6-9
SECOND READING: Ephesians 1:17-23
GOSPEL: Mark 16:15-20

In the Gospel today, Jesus sends His Disciples into the whole world to share His message, and then Jesus ascends into heaven right before their eyes.

It's been another great week here in Paradise! And not only because of the awesome sunshine and weather, and the mixed berry pie, and the box of deep fudge brownies, but because I get to celebrate with all of you this Memorial Day weekend.

35 years ago Monday, I was ordained a priest at Sacred Heart Cathedral in Newark, New Jersey. I was ordained by Bishop John J. Dougherty, the President of Seton Hall University. Archbishop Boland was supposed to ordain my class of 21 men, but ever since the unfortunate accident in which I had accidentally set him on fire by dropping a flaming piece of charcoal under his vestments, and then had accidentally nearly shoved him down a flight of stairs, my class was certain that he'd never let me get that near him again! So my classmates laughed when we learned at the last minute that Bishop Dougherty and not Archbishop

Boland would be ordaining us. During my college days, I had accidentally punched Bishop Dougherty in the face, but mercifully he didn't remember that it was I who had done it! So far Bishop Pepe is the only bishop I have been near whom I haven't accidentally physically harmed.

In these 35 years, I have married nearly 300 couples, baptized nearly 600 people, given 100's of First Holy Communions, anointed hundreds of those who were sick, heard thousands of confessions, and (as of Monday) celebrated 17423 Masses! I've worked as a high school teacher, chaplain, parish priest, pastor, Air Force chaplain, cruise ship chaplain, and parish administrator.

I've gotten to travel all over the world, and have celebrated Mass in Iceland, Turkey, Israel, Egypt, Germany, Holland, Austria, England, Macau, Tahiti, Australia, New Zealand, Venezuela, Hong Kong, the Virgin Islands, Bahamas, Bermuda, most of the 50 states, and even in St. Peter's Basilica in Rome. I've visited hospitals, prisons, nursing homes and insane asylums. I've been punched out by a guy who was really angry with God and I just happened to be wearing a Roman collar when he saw me. In my first parish in 1974, I followed 4 priests who had one after the other left the priesthood. The parish was named Our Lady of Lourdes, but was nicknamed Our Lady of the Revolving Door! I've been thinking about numbers a lot this week. I know it's weird to keep count of things like Masses and weddings and baptisms, but I like doing it.

No matter how many times I offer Mass, I never want to forget that offering each Mass is a tremendous gift from God. There's an old saying that a priest should celebrate every Mass as if it were his first Mass and as if it were his last Mass. I've always loved that thought.

Why am I boring you with all this rambling about what I remember? Well, I am firmly convinced that of all the gifts that God has given to us, the greatest gift (besides the Holy Eucharist which we celebrate at Mass today) is the GIFT OF MEMORY. God in His goodness allows us to remember. We can remember our phone numbers and zip codes, but most importantly, we can remember the people and places and events that are important and significant in our lives. This is a great gift!

One of the songs running through my mind at this time of year dates back to 1962 from the long-running musical "The Fantastiks." The song is "Try to Remember." I've loved that song ever since I first heard it. In fact, it was the son that was the theme of my high school senior prom back in 1966. And of course that reminded me of the girl I dated and took to the prom. On our first date, I was helping her into my car (a really classy 1960 Ford Station Wagon) and I slammed the door on her leg. Then, we stopped by her parents and her father asked me where we were going. Well, I was working at a church youth group project at Rockland State Psychiatric Hospital, so I told him that's where I was taking his daughter. All he asked was: "Will you bring her back?" Even the night of the prom was memorable. We double-dated with another couple and the guy from the other couple and I got into a fight. He was threatening to throw me into the reflecting pond at the Manor in West Orange when some chaperones came along and broke up the fight. And then, we had to ride home after the prom in the same car with him driving! All of that and so much more came back to me when I was thinking of "Try to Remember."

Memory is a great gift from God. That's why it's so much fun to remember the people and places and events in our lives. That's also why it is so important to remember what the Scriptures teach us about God and His incredible care for us.

Every Mass is for us a memorial, a remembrance of what God has done for us. Jesus even tells us at the consecration of every Mass - "Do this in memory of me." And Jesus really meant what He said. He told us that the bread and wine we offer at Mass are changed into the BODY AND BLOOD OF JESUS CHRIST through the words of the priest. This is one of our most significant and unique beliefs as Roman Catholics. We really do believe in the REAL PRESENCE OF JESUS CHRIST in the Holy Eucharist.

Several things come to mind because of this wonderful Catholic belief. We really believe that Jesus remains in our church buildings in our tabernacles 24/7 - 25 hours a day and 7 days a week. We really believe that as Roman Catholics in the state of grace we are allowed (encouraged) to receive God Himself in Holy Communion. And we believe that none of this would be possible without the existence of an ordained priesthood. And we really believe that Jesus Christ meant what He said when He told us that He would not abandon us, but would remain with us until the end of time. Today's celebration of the Ascension of the Lord is a reminder to our memories that Jesus has not left us alone, but has remained with us through His sacraments, through His church, and through the people who make up our lives.

This weekend's celebration of Memorial Day also calls us to remember. To remember the sacrifices of the men and women throughout our American history who have given their lives so that you and I could live in freedom. Their dedication to duty and honor and integrity is worth remembering. Our liberty comes at a price. May we also remember all those veterans who have served and survived in America's wars. And may we be mindful of those who currently serve in our ARMY, NAVY, AIR FORCE, MARINES and COAST GUARD in the war against terrorism today, especially those whose lives are at risk in Afghanistan and Iraq and other places around the world. We remember and we pray for all those who serve our nation.

As the refrain from "Try to Remember" says: "Try to remember and if you remember, then follow, follow, follow." May we remember and follow the faith and integrity of those who have gone before us as we remember them this Memorial Day weekend. And may we remember and follow the Faith in the Lord's Real Presence remaining with us in the Holy Eucharist.

I hope that our locals and visitors alike realize what an awesome community you are! We get to have Mass in our beautiful little church, and we get to have Mass in the casino showroom. We get to live in or to visit this Paradise on the banks of the beautiful Colorado River. And while you all need a priest in order to have this community of faith, be sure to remember that the priest needs you even more. Without you, and your enthusiasm, and your Faith, and your day-in and day-out caring for one another, we wouldn't have this community and this wouldn't be Paradise! I pray for you every day, and I'm counting on you praying for me!

This Mass is (4:00 PM) #17418, (8:00 AM) #17419, (10:00 AM) #17420, (Noon) #17421, (6:00 PM) #17422, one of the 497.8 Masses that I celebrate each year. I'm thrilled to be celebrating this Mass here with you in Laughlin. It really is Paradise here! I loved being a priest on May 25, 1974, when I was ordained. And 35 years later, I love it even more because of you! God bless you!

✤ ✤ ✤

Pentecost Sunday - "B"

31 May 2009

FIRST READING: Acts 2:1-11
PSALM: Psalm 104:1, 24, 29-31, 34
SECOND READING: 1 Corinthians 12:3b-7, 12-13
GOSPEL: John 20:19-23

In the Gospel today, Jesus promises His Holy Spirit to those who believe in Him.

What an amazing week this has been here in Paradise! Loved the celebration of my 35th anniversary as a priest last weekend even though I never thought I would survive the dancing! When my friend Michael yelled out: **"Give him a dollar for a dance!"**, I thought no one would pay attention to him. But the women lined up with dollars in their hands, and two men had to be pushed out of the line, and I kept hoping the music would slow down a little! But I made $63.00 on the dancing, and ended with dollar bills stuffed into each of my pockets.... and that includes a $20.00 bill one woman stuffed into my shirt as payment for NOT dancing with her! My legs were so sore the next morning! I was sure that when I genuflected in front of the altar that I would just stay down there! Nathan Burton is in town this week doing his magic show at Harrah's....so I went over to see it twice and loved it. Can never have too much good magic! And remember the American Madmen who were at the Pioneer during River Run with their sideshow and knife-throwing, money-stapling act? They posted a video of their Laughlin show on YouTube this week....and since I was standing right next to the stage for several of their shows, you can see my head in the video. I wonder if Bishop Pepe watches YouTube? I guess I'll find out.

As you may have guessed, I have a tendency to overdo things. If I open a bag of peanuts intending to only eat one, I know that very quickly I will be finished with most of the bag. If I see something on sale, I tend to buy not only one, but several just because they are such a good buy! I did that once at a farmers' market. Ripe cantaloupes were on sale for only 10 cents each. I bought a case of 30 of them! When I was telling my friends about it the next morning, they all had the same question: "What are you going to do with 30 ripe cantaloupes?" I did the same thing last year with shoes. A tuxedo rental store was closing and selling off its merchandise. They had brand new or hardly used black shoes for only $2.00 a pair! I couldn't pass it up, so now I have 7 pairs! (Hey, for $14.00 where could I get 7 pairs of shoes?!) And two months ago, Office Depot had a sale on pens, so I ended up buying 10 dozen of them. They were only $.50 a dozen! My only problem with this tendency to overdo things is that now I am running out of space to store my bargains!

And with the celebration of Pentecost, the tendency to overdo things is also present. I'd love to fill the church with reminders of the Holy Spirit. I checked and there are three main symbols of the Holy Spirit in the Scriptures. He is depicted as a DOVE (hovering over Jesus during His baptism in the Jordan River), as a FLAME OF FIRE (enlightening the minds of the Apostles on Pentecost), and as a WIND (sending the breath of God's life into creation). Of course, filling the church with DOVES, FLAMES and WIND would not be a really good idea! But one thought happily crossed my mind this week. See what you think of it. God is even more likely to overdo things than I am!

God gives to us so generously, generously beyond our belief. Look what He did for the Apostles on Pentecost in freeing them from fear and sending them out far and wide to all nations and peoples. Look at the different gifts and talents God has given to His people down through the ages. We all know people even today in our own parishes who face incredible hardships and difficulties with an amount of strength that can only come from God, not from themselves alone. God gives to us so generously even when we only ask for a little. God will not be outdone in generosity to us.

Today's Feast of Pentecost commemorates the fact that 50 days after Easter, Jesus sent the Holy Spirit upon the Apostles as a GIFT to strengthen them, to remove their fears, and to send them out on a mission. And while the Holy Spirit is the "Gift of the Father" to us, the Holy Spirit shares His presence and power with us in a variety of ways. The traditional **SEVEN GIFTS OF THE HOLY SPIRIT** remind us of some of those ways. I wonder how many of us actually remember them from our Catholic upbringing? Don't feel too badly.....I had to look them up myself to be sure!

WISDOM - helps us to understand more deeply the truths of our Faith. God, because He is good, wants us to know about Him. He shares His truth with us through our Catholic Faith.

UNDERSTANDING - helps us to see all created persons and things in their right relationship with God. Each human person is made in God's own image, even irrational creatures contain a "trace" of their Creator. Human events lead us towards God.

COUNSEL - God even shares with us His Divine guidance so we can truly know which actions and thoughts are right, and which actions and thoughts are wrong.

FORTITUDE - strengthens our will-power so that with God's help we can stick to doing what is right, and avoid doing what is wrong even when it is difficult, or burdensome, or boring to do so.

KNOWLEDGE - gives us a greater understanding of God and His love for us.

PIETY - helps us to want to be in union with God and to worship Him faithfully. It is this gift which encourages us to pray, to attend Mass, and to worship God.

FEAR OF THE LORD - produces in us a profound respect and reverence for God, and makes us want to avoid anything that would offend God. It is a healthy fear, a healthy respect, and it for our benefit to respect and have reverence for God.

Like any other GIFTS, the **SEVEN GIFTS OF THE HOLY SPIRIT** have to be received and have to be opened. We might wonder what is inside them, what they might do for us, but we actually have to open them and use them to really find out. We don't really know what this earth could be like if only we were to open up the **SEVEN GIFTS OF THE HOLY SPIRIT** and use them. All we do know is that God has promised us that with these gifts we can renew the face of the earth. Pray today that God's Holy Spirit may enlighten and strengthen each one of us, so that we can appreciate the great gifts we have received, and that we will open them and use them in our lives.

A survey was done a few years ago about the types of prayers that Americans pray. It discovered that 85% of all prayers were prayers asking God for things. GIVE ME THIS, GIVE ME THAT! I was really upset about that survey because it seemed to indicate that the only time we ever go to God is when we want something from Him. But the more I thought about it, the more it seemed to me that there is another way of looking at that statistic.

IF WE GO TO GOD TO ASK HIM FOR SOMETHING FOR OURSELVES OR FOR OUR NEIGHBORS, AREN'T

WE REALLY ADMITTING THAT WE NEED GOD, that we can't do it without Him? And doesn't today's Feast of Pentecost suggest that if we even open ourselves up to God's Spirit a little, God will give us so much more strength and help than we could ever ask for.

God overdoes things far more than you and I do. God will not be outdone in generosity. Today let us celebrate Pentecost by really asking God for what we most need in our lives, and may we really feel God's tremendous generosity in answering our prayers beyond our wildest expectations.

I may need a lot more storage space to hold my bargains, but even the whole world cannot contain all that God offers to us through His Holy Spirit.

God bless you!

The Most Holy Trinity - "B"

7 June 2009

FIRST READING: Deuteronomy 4:32-34, 39-40
PSALM: Psalm 33:4-6, 9, 18-20, 22
SECOND READING: Romans 8:14-17
GOSPEL: Matthew 28:16-20

In the Gospel today, Jesus teaches His Disciples that they must go out and share His teaching about the Father, and the Son, and the Holy Spirit.

My blood must have thinned out here in Paradise! I was on a retreat with the priests of the Diocese of Las Vegas up in Menlo Park, California, this week and I was freezing in my room! I was glad to get back to Laughlin where the air feels nice and warm! On the retreat, one of the priests asked where I was, and when I told him I was in Laughlin, he commented: "It's like hell down there!" **Good...that means he'll never be asking to come here so my plan is working! I don't want someone else to be eating the muffins and cashew brittle and homemade foods that I'm getting here!**

My friend Michael who was here for Memorial Day weekend is a professional singer and he got to hear me sing for the first time at Mass when I sang the **"Through Him, with Him, in Him..."** I asked Michael if he had any comments on my singing and he said he wanted to talk to me about it. He said that most other priests he's heard just sing in a monotone.... but, he said, **"You use notes!.....They aren't the right notes, but you use notes!"**

Years ago when I preached my very first sermon, I asked a priest/friend of mine to comment on it afterwards, and this is what he said to me: **"I have three things to say to you about it.....It was read, it was read poorly, and it wasn't worth reading!"** I guess I should learn never to ask a friend's opinion!

Any priest enjoys hearing favorable comments on his sermons. Some time ago, a parishioner came up to me to talk after one of the Masses. I thought that maybe I had said something which had particularly touched her heart, but she wasn't impressed with my theological clarity! She just wanted to tell me: **"You're so funny. Whenever I see you walking towards the pulpit, I start to laugh before you even open your mouth! Thank you for brightening my week!"** I guess there's some compliment in that! We preachers do reach people in different ways!

And God reaches us in a variety of ways too! Today's feast is called TRINITY SUNDAY, a day on which we celebrate the MYSTERY OF THE HOLY TRINITY - THE MYSTERY OF THREE PERSONS IN ONE GOD. It's a mystery because we don't fully understand it, but we do experience it, and every Sunday we say in the CREED that we believe in the FATHER, and in the SON, and in the HOLY SPIRIT. We experience God in our lives in many ways that reflect the TRINITY.

God is a loving and caring parent, a Father in the truest and most beautiful sense of the word. He created the world and He holds it in existence. He is all-powerful.

God is Jesus, a true human being, a person like us in all things but sin, a warm and personal friend to each one of us. He is close to us.

God is the Holy Spirit, an all-pervading Presence, a power who enlightens our minds and strengthens our wills to do good and to avoid evil. He is God's gift of wisdom to each one of us.

Each one of us has his/her own way of relating to God or thinking about God. The TRINITY reminds us that we all need to relate to God in His WHOLENESS. He is a loving and caring Father, but He is also an AWESOME JUDGE who controls the entire universe. In Jesus, He is a truly human person like us, but he is NEVER "just like us." He is always God among us. As the Holy Spirit, He is God's wisdom in the world, but He works through us and through others to share His wisdom and guidance. We need to pay attention to Him when He opens doors in our lives through people and events around us.

God is greater and larger than any of our categories for Him. He is beyond our categories of time and space. He is the God Who created the world, Who freed His people from slavery at the time of Moses, Who has in our own time chosen us as His own sons and daughters, and Who shares His own Spirit with us. He will remain with us always.

The simple sign of the cross which we make so often (and sometimes so carelessly) is a powerful reminder that God always remains a mystery to us. He is Someone greater than we can ever imagine, Someone Who cannot be confined to our narrow categories and our very limited minds. God has made each one of us in His own image. We should never reverse things and try to make our God just like us.

God is higher, deeper and wider than even the universe itself.....and for some reason in His eternal plan, God wants to be close to us! Think of that the next time you make the sign of the cross. God wants to be close to you!

In the Name of the Father, and of the Son, and of the Holy Spirit. Amen.

God bless you!

Corpus Christi - "B"

14 June 2009

FIRST READING: Exodus 24:3-8
PSALM: Psalm 116:12-13, 15-18
SECOND READING: Hebrews 9:11-15
GOSPEL: Mark 14:12-16, 22-26

In the Gospel today, Jesus at the Last Supper gives His Apostles His own Body and Blood to strengthen them for their journey through life.

Another great week in Paradise! The weather is warming up so summer cannot be far behind. I heard that Oatman is planning a "cook an egg on the sidewalk" contest. Just one more good reason to love it out here! A friend came over to try to spike my hair so I'd look more in tune with the times. After he convinced me to put some mousse in my hair and started grabbing it into little clumps, I looked in the mirror and thought I resembled a mangy dog who had lost a fight! I don't think I have enough hair up there for spiking! Sat down to play $20 on a favorite penny slot here at the Riverside, hit a bonus round, and walked away with over $223.00. **You gotta love this place!**

Father Peter took me out to lunch, one of the parishioners bought me dinner, and I've enjoyed the banana bread and Bananas Foster that came my way this week. Not to mention the fried peppers and a whole basket filled with Polish pickles and jams and candies. I got no sleep on my day off up in Vegas. My friend Michael is going to New York to take a three-month personal trainer course so Eddie and I took him out for a "Last Supper" and then we stayed up until almost 5:00 AM talking and looking at old pictures from our families. We ended up sitting on the floor like two little kids fighting to stay awake! **So as long as we were on our knees, we ended the night by praying.** Even found some lost coins on the carpet. I am so blessed out here!

On Saturday, June 13th, we celebrated the Feast of St. Anthony of Padua, a Franciscan who lived in the 1200's. Because of some of the miracles attributed to him, St. Anthony even today is invoked as the patron saint of finding lost articles. Some might even remember a rhyme learned as little children: **"St. Anthony, St. Anthony, please come around. Something is lost and cannot be found."** I have to admit a certain tendency on my part to just blindly keep looking for lost objects (like my sunglasses, or my checkbook, or a phone number on a scrap of paper) until I get really desperate, and then I revert to the old ways, and just give up and call on St. Anthony. Amazingly, he normally comes through! But St. Anthony is also invoked as a patron saint against starvation, so it is appropriate that we remember his feast as we celebrate the feast of CORPUS CHRISTI, the BODY AND BLOOD OF CHRIST. I think it is a safe assumption on my part that there is probably no one else you know who enjoys talking about food more than I do. I love eating and I love eating out. (And, no, that is not a cheap hint for more gift certificates!) I never want recipes! I don't want to know how to prepare the food. I just want to know people who know how to prepare the food! I love pasta and cheese and ice cream and cake and fresh bread and chocolate chip cookies. Now I'm getting myself hungry! I like the feeling of being contentedly full!

There's no doubt about it, my friends, food and drink do affect us. There's even a wonderful old saying: **"You are what you eat."** Of course, when I think of some of the food that I've consumed over the years.....the peanut butter and banana pizzas, the cold egg rolls with hot mustard for breakfast, the garlic ice cream, even the three-day old reheated coffee, that particular saying can be frightening!

But down through the ages, God has come to mankind through food. Just think about it.....ADAM and EVE were placed in a garden. JOSEPH stored the grain in Egypt to provide for his people in a time of great famine. MOSES fed the Israelites with manna (bread) from heaven after they had left Egypt. JESUS fed thousands of people with only a little bread and fish. And JESUS left us the Holy Eucharist, His own Body and Blood, in the form of bread and wine.

On this warm and beautiful weekend, I'd like to just suggest three simple reasons why I think God acted in this way throughout history, choosing to come to us down through the ages in signs connected with food. Here they are:

1. Because God knows our fascination with food. Almost all of our celebrations are somehow connected with food. Try to even imagine Christmas or Easter or Thanksgiving or a birthday or an anniversary without food! Even a funeral includes a repast after the burial. When we come together in joy or in sorrow, we like to eat together.

2. Because God wants to remind us that we need Him daily, even day. None of us does without food for any great length of time. If supper is ten minutes late, we complain that we're STARVING!

3. Maybe because God really believes that wonderful old saying I mentioned - **"YOU ARE WHAT YOU EAT!"** Think about that one this week. Maybe God wants us to become more like He is! That's why we don't eat or drink anything else for an hour before receiving Holy Communion. That's why we don't receive Holy Communion if we're living in a state of serious sin. That's why we make use of the Sacrament of Confession to get ourselves out of that state of serious sin. Because in receiving Holy Communion, we are invited by God Himself to become like He is.

If you are fortunate enough to be able to receive Holy Communion today, just think about what God is inviting you to become - united with Him, united with God Who is the Source of all holiness. God couldn't possibly give us a greater gift than Himself. He literally puts Himself into our hands as well as into our bodies. God Himself joins Himself to us in a way that is possible only through receiving the BODY AND BLOOD OF JESUS CHRIST in the form of bread and wine.

This is why we gather every Sunday. This is why there is a priesthood. This really is why we are Catholic. The Holy Eucharist, the Body and Blood of Christ, is only available to us here. We have nothing more important to offer to you than the opportunity to be physically united with God Himself in Holy Communion. May we daily become more like God. **"You are what you eat!"** In receiving Holy Communion, we pray that this may really be true.

God bless you!

12th Sunday in Ordinary Time - "B"

21 June 2009

FIRST READING: Job 38:1, 8-11
PSALM: Psalm 107:23-26, 28-31
SECOND READING: 2 Corinthians 5:14-17
GOSPEL: Mark 4:35-41

In the Gospel today Jesus calms a violent storm out on the waters, and He reassures His disciples of His constant care for them.

What an exciting week here in Paradise! I spent Monday night in the emergency room at WARMC! Oh, not for me.....it was for Pat, my secretary visiting from New Jersey. **Intense pains in her left shoulder.** At 11:30 PM, she called and told me she had dialed 911 and thought she was having a heart attack. After six hours, the doctor told her that it wasn't a heart attack. Seems that Pat is left-handed, and the slot machine handles are on the right side. So for the past month while she was working here at St. John the Baptist, she has been stretching her shoulder muscles more than back home in New Jersey. He said the technical term for her condition was **"slot machine arm!"** A little muscle relaxant and some pain meds and Pat was fine. Now that's a story she'll take home and share!

I discovered an interesting statistic. There are more collect phone calls on Father's Day than on any other day in the year. I guess fathers like hearing from their children even when they have to pay for it. I always remember back in my first parish in the 1970's complaining to the First Graders in the parish school that even though everyone calls me "FATHER", I never get a Father's Day card. One First Grader explained it to me: "You're not the right kind of father!" So to all of you who are the "right kind" of fathers, grandfathers, step-fathers, Godfathers, etc. I wish you the best possible day for Father's Day. And I can no longer say that I've never gotten a Father's Day card! My friend Eddie (who is nicknamed my illegitimate son....long story!) gave me a Father's Day card this week. It's my first one ever! It brought a tear to my eye as I read it: **"Dad, I love you for more reasons than there are stars in the sky, more reasons than there are grains of sand on the beach, more reasons than there are hairs on your head...okay, maybe that last one is not such a good comparison! Happy Father's Day!"**

I love today's Gospel with the disciples crowded in the boat with Jesus as the storm comes up and Jesus is sound asleep on a cushion. The disciples wake Him up asking: "Do you not care that we are perishing?" So Jesus gets up, rebukes the wind and the sea, and it all gets really calm. And then He asks the disciples: "Why are you terrified? Do you not yet have faith?" Even the disciples of Jesus found it hard to believe that God care for and protected them. And sometimes you and I need to be convinced of that too. We need to have faith that God cares, and that we're worth a lot to Him.

A popular speaker started off a seminar by holding up a crisp new $20 bill. "Who would like this $20 bill?", he asked. Hands went up all over the room. He said, "I am going to give this $20 bill to one of you, but first let me do this." He then crumpled the bill up in his hand. Then he asked again, "Who still wants it?" And all the hands went up again. "Well," he said, "what if I do this?" And he dropped the $20 bill on the floor and started to grind it into the dirt on the floor with his shoe. He picked it up, now all crumpled and dirty and torn, and asked, "Who still wants it?" And all the hands went up again. And then he concluded:

"My friends, you have learned a valuable lesson. No matter what I did to the money, you still wanted it because it did not decrease in value. It was still worth $20. Many times in our lives, we are dropped, crumpled, and even ground into the dirt by the decisions we make, or others make, or by the circumstances of our lives. We might even feel as though we are close to worthless. **BUT NO MATTER WHAT HAS HAPPENED OR WHAT WILL HAPPEN, YOU WILL NEVER LOSE YOUR VALUE IN THE EYES OF GOD, OUR FATHER.** To Him, dirty or clean, crumpled or finely creased, you are still precious and valuable. God loves us and sees us as always valuable and precious in His eyes."

Father's Day is today. Summer begins this week. As we go about our lives, fathers, mothers and all of us should never forget the message of today's Gospel: God cares for us, and we're worth a lot to Him. Why is it so hard for us to have faith in that?

God bless you!

Proud Father Charlie and bearded son Eddie!
(Ask the locals for the explanation!)

13th Sunday in Ordinary Time - "B"

28 June 2009

FIRST READING: Wisdom 1:13-15; 2:23-24
PSALM: Psalm 30:2, 4-6, 11-13
SECOND READING: 2 Corinthians 8:7, 9, 13-15
GOSPEL: Mark 5:21-43

In the Gospel today, Jesus works two amazing cures because of the very evident faith of those who seek out His help.

What an amazing week in Paradise! Besides the usual array of awesome foods, including a wonderful gnocchi with chicken and kalamata olives, **I got to meet the Governor of Nevada.** He was in Laughlin on Tuesday and I was invited to pray at the luncheon here at the Riverside. In the invocation, I told him that we were glad to welcome him to Paradise, and he picked up on it later during his talk. So now the Governor of Nevada agrees with me that this really is Paradise! **There really is an old, but obscure, scientific theory proclaimed by Alan LeBaron that the Garden of Eden was located right here where Laughlin now stands.** I'm researching it, and will be reporting back on it later in the summer.

We celebrated becoming a parish on Wednesday night with over 100 people at the church (and a delicious cake!) Two friends of mine appeared on the Tonight Show on Thursday night, so I had to stay up to see them. For those who watch the Tonight

Show, I'll let you guess which two of the guests were my friends.

Some visitors to Laughlin last month accidentally took their slot tickets home with them to Wisconsin, and since they had come to church with us, they had our bulletin at home. So they mailed us their slot tickets as a donation to the church. Actually lots of people do that, and we're really grateful for it. But these tickets added up to over $300.00! So, everyone, please take home a copy of our bulletin.....just in case.

And I decided to play my Zeus machine on Friday night. played for a few minutes, hit a big bonus round, and walked away with $1000.00. I love this place!

On Saturday, July 4th, we will celebrate the 233rd Birthday of our great American nation. I don't need to give a long sermon today, and you don't need to sit through one. But I thought I'd point out a little inspiration for this week as we prepare to celebrate our 233rd Birthday as a free and independent nation. And I found this inspiration in two sources: The Declaration of Independence and today's Gospel Reading from St. Mark.

The Declaration of Independence, which was signed 233 years ago this week, begins with these words:

"We hold these truths to be self-evident, that all men are created equal, that they are endowed by

their Creator with certain unalienable Rights, that among these are Life, Liberty and the Pursuit of Happiness."

233 year later, we all need to remember that from the very beginning, our nation has acknowledged that there is a **CREATOR**, and that He is the Source of all our rights. And that we are all endowed by our Creator with the right to **LIFE**, and to **LIBERTY**, and to the **PURSUIT OF HAPPINESS**. The Declaration of Independence states that all of this is **SELF-EVI-DENT**, meaning that any thinking person should be able to see it.

So as we prepare to celebrate July 4th next week-end, it's good for us to give thanks to our **CREATOR**, and to thank Him for giving us **LIFE**, and **LIBERTY**, and for allowing us to pursue **HAPPINESS**. It should be **SELF-EVIDENT** to all of us that God has given us so much in the course of our lives. It's good to think about this.

In today's Gospel from St. Mark, the faith of two people is also SELF-EVIDENT. Jairus, the synagogue leader, comes to Jesus because he really believes that Jesus has the power to heal his very sick daughter. And the unnamed woman, who had been sick for 12 years, really believes that if she could just get close enough to Jesus to touch His clothing, she would be cured.

Many centuries later as we look back at their faith, it should be **SELF-EVIDENT** to us that in their desperation both Jairus and that woman came to Jesus because they knew that there was no other place to go, no other person to turn to who could help them.

And that's what should be so inspirational to us today. We live in a country where we can freely come to God in worship. And like Jairus and the unnamed woman in today's Gospel, we know that He has something to offer us that no one else has. He can help us in ways that no one else can. It's good to think about this too. It should be **SELF-EVIDENT** that it makes good sense to be close to God.

In today's Gospel, when Jesus says, "Do not be afraid, just have faith," He is talking as much to each one of us as to the people in the Gospel. May God bless each one of us with the **SELF-EVIDENT FAITH** we see in today's Gospel.

God bless you!

14 Sunday in Ordinary Time - "B"

5 July 2009

FIRST READING: Ezekiel 2:2-5
PSALM: Psalm 123:1-4
SECOND READING: 2 Corinthians 12:7-10
GOSPEL: Mark 6:1-6a

In the Gospel today, Jesus comes home to His own town of Nazareth, but He is not well-received by the townsfolk who feel they know where He is from and how limited His background is.

Another awesome week in Paradise! Temperatures hit 115 degrees one day this week, so we're finally warming up a bit! Enjoyed some homemade ravioli stuffed with spinach and cheese, some angelfood cake layered with sherbet, and an amazing grilled chicken citrus salad. Played some cards with some parishioners (and lost!). Got asked to bless a fish, and to bury a horse. And even turned down an invitation by David Copperfield to attend a movie. But it was at midnight and I really wanted to get some sleep. How many folks ever get to say that they turned down an invitation from David Copperfield?

And I got visited by a priest and some members of a religious group from out of state. They came for Mass and then we talked, and they promised to pray for me. After I thanked them, they said they would be praying for me to have courage since I had to live here with all this sin! They had visited a casino in Laughlin and told me that they saw **"all those pathetic old people putting money into machines and they don't know God!"** My immediate response was **"Those pathetic old people are my parishioners!"** But then I gave a better defense! My experience here in Laughlin has been different. I don't feel that I'm surrounded by sin, and I certainly don't feel like I have to deal with pathetic old people who don't know God! **So I just smiled and knew that as I begin my second year here that there's one more priest who doesn't want to take my place, and eat my food, and have all this fun with my parishioners in Paradise!** So if anyone ever tells you that it's boring to be a priest, have them come and talk with me. That was my week!

I love to travel and sometimes I get to meet some amazing people along the way. Back in 2006 while I was in New Jersey, I got an email which began: "Do you believe in magic? Do you believe in miracles? You don't know who this is now, but you will at the end of this email." Well, it sounded like one of those chain letters. But I read on: "Do you remember being at the Gold River Casino in Laughlin, Nevada, in August, 1997?" Now I'm thinking this might be an attempt at blackmail! But I read on: "You came to see my magic show and wrote me a letter telling me how much you enjoyed it. I just got your letter this week - nine years later!" The letter had fallen behind some furniture and was only discovered by an employee who happened to have worked there all these years. He was able to track down the magician to whom my letter had been addressed. He had moved back to Massachusetts to care for his Dad who had had a stroke and was in the beginning stages of alzheimer's. The magician whose stage name is FLASH had checked on the Internet and found that I was still at the same parish in New Jersey. A few weeks later, after a lot of emails and talking on the phone, we got to meet each other. We went out for dinner and stayed up until 4:30 AM the next morning talking about Las Vegas and Laughlin and magic and our lives. I like to think that God had this all planned out when our paths had crossed nine years earlier here in Laughlin, Nevada, so that we could meet up in 2006 on the East Coast. And being able to share with each other about his Dad and my Mom both having alzheimer's was really great for both of us. Flash was in town this week, and we had a great time up in Vegas for two days. This is just one of my TRAVEL STORIES.....and I've got thousands more!

I REALLY LOVE TO TRAVEL, and I suspect that Jesus loved to travel too. So many of the Gospels are about His journeys throughout Judea, Samaria and Galilee. They tell us of the cures He worked, the people He visited, the teachings He gave in the various places throughout the ancient land of Israel. But today's Gospel is different. Jesus comes HOME to His own area, to His own hometown, to His own place of worship. If we were reading this Gospel passage for the first time, we might logically expect that here in Nazareth Jesus would work His greatest miracles. But exactly the opposite is true. Jesus did very little in the way of preaching or teaching or curing the sick in His own hometown. In St. Mark's words in the Gospel today, "So he was not able to perform any mighty deed there, apart from curing a few sick people by laying His hands on them. He was amazed at their lack of faith." I suspect that it was not that they people lacked the will to have faith, it was that they couldn't bring themselves to have faith in someone so close.

So often, I think, we have the same problem as the people of Nazareth in today's Gospel. It's easy to believe in God when He's kept at a distance, and it's easy to love someone we don't see very often. (We even have a proverb: **"Absence makes the heart grow fonder"** or the famous Charlie Brown saying: **"I love humanity...it's people I can't stand!"** But, sometimes, I think, the reason we see so little good going on around us in our country, in our own town, in our own neighborhood, or in our own family, is that we really look for it so faithlessly. WE REALLY DON'T EXPECT our children to be terrific. We really don't expect our parents to be understanding. We really don't think we'll see or hear great wisdom from the local valet parking attendant, a store clerk, a local teacher, an ex-convict, or our next door neighbor. The sad part of all this is that since we expect so little, we see so little. And we can go through our lives missing a lot of the good things and the good people around us. We can even miss God Himself in our midst. After all, the people of Nazareth didn't see Who Jesus really was. Sometimes we still take God for granted. We come late or carelessly to His Eucharist. We leave early because we have something more important to do than spend a few more minutes with God. We bend and twist God's teachings to suit our own convenience. And, sadly, the result is still the same as it was in Nazareth some 2000 years ago....Jesus could work no miracles there so much did their lack of faith distress Him.

Beginning today, maybe we can come to appreciate Jesus and His message a little bit more. Maybe we can recognize Him better in His Word, in the Eucharist, in His people, and in the good that He really tries to do around us and through us. we are, after all, on this 4th of July weekend, ONE NATION UNDER GOD, and we still have a chance to notice what Nazareth overlooked. Let's not miss it!

God bless you!

May 25th is Father Charlie's Anniversary of Ordination to the Priesthood.

18230734R00156

Made in the USA
Charleston, SC
23 March 2013